52 WEEKLY Devotions for BUSY FAMILIES

Karen Whiting

52 WEEKLY Devotions for BUSY FAMILIES

Karen Whiting

An imprint of Rose Publishing, Inc.
Carson, CA
www.Rose-Publishing.com

Dedication:

To my children and their families that they will continue to serve the Lord and enjoy sharing God's Word with their families.

- Karen Whiting

52 WEEKLY DEVOTIONS FOR BUSY FAMILIES
Copyright © 2016 Karen Whiting
ISBN 13: 978-16286-2508-0
ISBN 10: 1628625082
RoseKidz® reorder: #L50001

RoseKidz®
An imprint of Rose Publishing, Inc.
17909 Adria Maru Lane
Carson, CA 90746

Register your book at www.Rose-Publishing.com/register. Get free bible charts via email, sign up at www.Rose-Publishing.com.
Unless otherwise indicated, Scripture quotations are taken from the New International Reader's Version of the Bible, Copyright © 1995, 1996, 1998, 2014 by Biblica, Inc.® Used by permission. All rights reserved worldwide.

Verses marked NIV are taken from the New International Version (NIV) Holy Bible, New International Version®, NIV® Copyright © 1973, 1978, 1984, 2011 by Biblica, Inc.® Used by permission. All rights reserved worldwide.

Cover and interior design by Nancy L. Haskins
Illustrations by Katerina Davidenko

Published in association with Books & Such Literary Management,
52 Mission Circle, Suite 122, PMB 170
Santa Rosa, Ca 95409-5370

www.booksandsuch.com

Printed in China   01   12.2016.AP

Table of Contents

Letter to Parents 7

Family Devotion Tips and Benefits 9

WEEK 1: New Year's Week: Creation 15

WEEK 2: Belonging to Our Family 19

WEEK 3: What's in a Name? 23

WEEK 4: Affection 27

WEEK 5: Who is God? 31

WEEK 6: Valentine's Week: Praise and Encouragement 35

WEEK 7: Talking to God? 39

WEEK 8: Lent: Hearing God 43

WEEK 9: Personalities 47

WEEK 10: T-I-M-E Spells Love 51

WEEK 11: Listen! 55

WEEK 12: Adventures in Learning 59

WEEK 13: Easter: Treasuring Easter 63

WEEK 14: Understanding 67

WEEK 15: Approval 71

WEEK 16: Spring: Hope 75

WEEK 17: Success 79

WEEK 18: Trust 83

WEEK 19: Overcoming Fears 87

WEEK 20: Fresh Starts 91

WEEK 21: Discipline 95

WEEK 22: Summer: Summer Fun 99

WEEK 23: Money Sense 103

WEEK 24: Life Skills 107

WEEK 25: July 4th: Patriotism 111

WEEK 26: Politeness 115

WEEK 27: The Great Outdoors 119

WEEK 28: Work Ethic 123

WEEK 29: Responsibility 127

WEEK 30: Cooperation 131

WEEK 31: Sprinkles of Joy 135

WEEK 32: Back to School: Knowledge 139

WEEK 33: Comfort 143

WEEK 34: Autumn: Fall Fun 147

WEEK 35: World Views 151

WEEK 36: Understanding Messages 155

WEEK 37: Service 159

WEEK 38: Friendships 163

WEEK 39: Priorities 167

WEEK 40: Respect Life Month: Convictions 171

WEEK 41: Generosity 175

WEEK 42: Following God 179

WEEK 43: Sharing Your Faith 183

WEEK 44: Temptation and Sin 187

WEEK 45: Making Decisions 191

WEEK 46: Thanksgiving: Thanksgiving 195

WEEK 47: Failure 199

WEEK 48: Advent: Thoughtfulness 203

WEEK 49: Stress 207

WEEK 50: Fairness and Justice 211

WEEK 51: Christmas: Celebrating Jesus 215

WEEK 52: Winter Fun 219

Dear Parents,

I have five children. Looking back, I realize that our family devotions were the foundation of our family and the glue that held us together. We discovered hope as we studied Nehemiah during our home's reconstruction. We stayed close during many military deployments knowing my husband and our children's dad was reading the same devotional we were using at home.

We launched our children into the world with biblical principles and brought them to know Jesus through readings in the New Testament. Each book of the Bible reminds me of ways the Word and our related activities strengthened us as a family.

Family time doesn't need to be boring or formal. We laughed when we acted out passages, enjoyed science experiments to investigate truths (for example, studying the effects of yeast), and used Christmas stockings to celebrate passages on the gifts of the Holy Spirit.

I encourage you to start with simple, familiar Scripture verses. Spend only a few moments studying with little ones. Let the time lengthen and the study grow deeper as children grow and their minds develop. There are challenges, especially during the teen years when children are going in so many directions. But it is worth forging ahead to grow your children in the Word. Continue to schedule time for family devotions. You'll build memories and strong bonds.

Let God's word light the pathway for your family.

Blessings,
Karen Whiting

> *"Your word is a lamp for my feet, a light on my path."*
> – Psalm 119:105 NIV

HOW: Start Simple

S Schedule time to gather together

I Involve your children

M Mix in fun and hands-on experiences

P Plan ahead and choose what you'll do before each week starts

L Let it become a legacy with capturing the memories

E End each one with prayer

Be Ready and Willing to Go the Distance

- Be committed
- Be consistent
- Be open-minded to children's responses and guide them to truth
- Be enthusiastic
- Be flexible
- Be realistic and understand your child's ability
- Be in the Word yourself so you know the Bible

Family Devotions Your Way

Let the family decide how they want to proceed. Some weeks are harder than others. On some days, there may only be time to read the devotion and do a few chats throughout the week. You can put out supplies for family members to do an activity as they have time. Check in with them when you wrap up the week.

Let this time together fit your family's lifestyle. Some weeks are relaxed, while others may be hectic and full.

Commit to one time each week as the launch day and one time to wrap the study up. Choose activities to fit the other days, a la carte when necessary.

Create a Family Devotion Scrapbook/Prayer Journal.

Each Devotion Week includes:

☐ A Bible story and related Bible verses to read and explore
☐ 1 short devotion to read and reflect on together
☐ 3 or more activities to choose from
☐ 2 or more ideas to add to your scrapbook/prayer journal
☐ 3 or more optional Chat Prompts: Options, usually paired with a scripture, related to the focus
☐ Wrap-up to discuss what family members learned about the topic and how the activities helped them

Choose Your Family Style:

☐ Choose your beginning
☐ If desired, start with an activity to introduce the concept and then read the devotions, or
☐ Start with the devotion, or
☐ Start with a scripture and chat prompt, or
☐ Add what looks doable that week

Activities and Chat Prompts: Options

Don't try to do every activity every week. Choose what fits your family best. You can always go through the book again in a year or two and use different activities.

Bible Story Connections

Part of doing devotions as a family is studying the truths in the Bible. Make this exploration fun by engaging all the senses. Use the suggested visuals and actions. Act out stories or retell them in your own words.

If one parent has a job that includes frequent travel:

- Buy 2 copies of this book—one for the family at home and one for the absent person.
- Record sessions for the absent parent.
- Do some activities and chats together using technology.
- Take photos to share to help bridge the distance.
- Have the absent parent email or text insights on the week's topic.

Scrapbook/Prayer Journal

Create a scrapbook/prayer journal to help your famiy reflect and remember each weeks "Aha" moments. You can buy a drawing or scrap book, a journal or just staple sheets of paper together. Each week look for the suggestions on how to reflect and add memories to your scrapbook.

- Let children add dabs of watercolor and then add a drawing or stamp design around them.
- Write in words that became buzz words during your study week.
- Add fun stickers that relate to the week's theme.
- Print and use graphite paper to add designs.
- Jazz the pages up to express how your family responded to the topic.
- Take photos of activities and add them to the pages.

Prayer

Use the prayer throughout the week. Read it each day at meals or bedtime. Make copies and keep them handy for on-the-go moments. Keep track of prayer requests and answered prayers in your Scrapbook/Prayer Journal.

Wrap-ups

End each week with a brief time to chat about the topic and activities. Ask what each person learned and add those thoughts to the pages of your scrapbook /prayer journal.

Start (or Restart) Any Week!

Don't wait for a new year to start family devotions. Start this week. Any time of year is a great time to start:

- Easter and new hope
- Spring and planting seed of faith
- Summer with a less rigid calendar
- Fall and the start of school
- Christmas or the New Year for new birth and new starts

1. As parents, read the opening and letter to parents.
2. If this is a restart, or you need motivation to persist, consider writing down from the list of benefits the three top reasons you want to succeed at family devotions and post those somewhere very visible for your family. Let those be your motivation or mottos to keep going.
3. Turn to the current week and get going!

Get Kids Excited About Devotions

1. Talk the devotions up.

Bring the devotion ideas into family mealtimes and drive times. Chat about the scriptures, talks, and activities.

2. Capture the fun in pictures.

Be sure to take photos of the activities when possible and build a family memory keepsake by adding the suggested art, thoughts, and photos to the scrapbook/prayer journal.

3. Engage the senses.

Use visuals and sounds affiliated with stories to tap into a sight, sound, and touch for deepening the impact. Act out passages. Why not cook foods that relate to Bible times? This helps children experience and understand Bible times.

4. Pray with a prayer cup.

Decorate a plastic cup with permanent makers. Cut slips of paper and write the names of each family member on one. At the end of each devotion, let each member draw a name to pray for that person. Or you can have someone draw one name at a meal and then, as a family, pray for that individual. If desired, add names of other family members and friends to pray for them too.

5. Connect with one-on-one time.

Consider doing some activities with one child at a time. Children love this special bonding time with a parent.

6. Memorize the week's opening scripture.

Read the verse daily and talk about what it means. After a few days, say some of the words and see if they can finish the verse. Recite it together. Look up fun memory verse games online.

7. Provide each child with his or her own age-appropriate Bible.

Having their own Bibles helps increase their interest. You can also provide journals or prayer notebooks. Match these items to your children's ages and learning styles. Visual learners want more pictures and charts; analytical children enjoy charts and facts; social learners like profiles about people and places.

8. Share what you learn.

Invite friends to join you for some of the devotions. Share the memories and how the devotion time helps your children and you grow in faith and other areas.

Before You Start:

Just a reminder to find a way that your family can create a Scrapbook/Prayer Journal.

Low/No Cost Option: Use the corners of this book or staple pieces of paper together. Label it "Family Devotions Scrapbook/ Prayer Journal. Each week suggestions will be given to add to this book. From time to time look back over what you have done together as a family.

Review God's faithfulness with prayer requests and answers. This will be a special reminder of this journey for years.

Busy Families

Each week look over all the activity and chat prompt options in each section.

Pick what fits your schedule that week. Those weeks you find yourself with extra time, check out the MORE TIME options. It is important to just seek to look for moments in everyday life to explore God together. You will feel the blessing of God over your family for your effort.

Creation

> **Family Beatitude:** Happy is the family who celebrates new starts, for they will have hope.
>
> **Focus:** Celebrating new starts
>
> **Weekly Bible Verse:** *"You were taught to start living a new life. It is created to be truly good and holy, just as God is."* – Ephesian 4:24

Family Activity Options

☐ No matter what time of year it is, you can start a new tradition. Start your family scrapbook/prayer journal and add your family's memories and hopes. Reflect on the past year to add memories. Write down praises and prayer requests. Include hopes and dreams for the future. Add anything special your family wants to record.

☐ Try making or buying a new food. It could be a dessert, snack, or main dish.

☐ Take a family walk and explore nature. Talk about any changes coming in the next few months. Discuss positive changes you can make as a family.

☐ Pray together for the coming year. Hold hands and form a prayer circle. Let the person who starts squeeze the hand of the next person when he or she is done. If someone wants to say a silent prayer, that's okay. Just have that person squeeze the next hand when ready. When the squeeze returns to the person who started the prayer, he or she can say, "Amen."

Celebrating New Beginnings

2 minutes

"It's time!" yelled Michael.

Michael's family gathered for their New Year's Day group hug and giggled. Then they launched into special activities to start their year.

Mom opened the special journal they added to once a year. She was ready to capture memories of the year that had just ended. Dad asked, "What are the funniest memories of the past year?" Previous years had included one child riding a horse that wouldn't budge until finally trotting the wrong way and the surprise of a new baby coming.

They also added the worst family memories, often an illness or disaster, such as lightning striking the house. They reviewed last year's prayer requests and noted the many prayer answers. Next, each person stated his or her praises to God from the past year and shared a prayer request for the coming year:

- "Help me not fight and complain so much."
- "Thanks for the new Bible Club at school."
- "Pray that I find a summer job."
- "Help me use my indoor voice when I'm inside."

This family keepsake journal contains memories of the years, answered prayers, and hopes for the future.

Michael's family continued the day with gifts of new books and educational games to enrich their minds; new foods for their bodies; and new plans for the family, including family devotion ideas for the coming months.

Michael said at the end of the day, "Now I feel like we've started a new year."

Bible Story Connection 3-4 minutes

Read how God created the world in Genesis 1. Pass out clay and
fashion animals. Chat about creation. Help them find which day
their favorite creation was made.

Chat Prompts: Options

● *"In the beginning, God created the heavens and the earth."*

– Genesis 1:1

Talk about new beginnings and the excitement of new starts. Set
goals and in the Scrapbook/Prayer Journal write down the steps
in your action plan to implement new ideas or challenges for this
week or longer.

MORE TIME?

● *"Sing a new song to [the Lord]. Play with skill, and shout
with joy."* – Psalm 33:3

Play or sing a new song. Chat about the joy that music brings
and the fun of discovering new songs. Let each person name
a favorite song.

● *"[The Lord says,] 'I will give my people hearts that are
completely committed to me. I will give them a new spirit that
is faithful to me. I will remove their stubborn hearts from them.
And I will give them hearts that obey me.' "* – Ezekiel 11:19

Share your testimonies of faith in Jesus. Talk about how hope
in Him renews your hearts.

● *"Like newborn babies, you should long for the pure milk of
God's word. It will help you grow up as believers."*

– 1 Peter 2:2

Chat about the plan to use this devotion book to take a new
look at God's Word and studying it as a family.

Scrapbook/Prayer Journal Options

Add art that illustrates fresh starts and creation.

- Use watercolors or colored pencils to paint some flowers, stars, and creatures.

- Add a dove for hope and write some hopes and prayer requests for the year.

- Add musical notes with notes of praises from the past year.

Prayer

Creator, thank you for the world you made and for placing each of us in this family. Help us grow closer to you and to each other this year.

Wrap Up

Chat about each person's plans and hopes for the coming year. Discuss ways to follow through.

Belonging to Our Family

Family Beatitude: Happy is the family who celebrates each member, so he or she will develop a sense of belonging.

Focus: Belonging

Weekly Bible Verse: " *'At that time I will be the God of all the families of Israel,' announces the Lord. 'And they will be my people.'* "

– Jeremiah 31:1

Activity Options on Belonging

☐ Take out baby books or family albums and chat about each person. Take a new family photo on your phone or with a camera and talk about resemblances in looks and behaviors.

☐ Write letters and notes to each other giving reasons why you are happy that person is part of the family. Focus on one person each day.

☐ Make a sign with your family name. Add hearts, each one bearing a family member's name. Hang it inside your home.

New Baby 1 minute

"It's Daniel's first New Year."

"He's still a baby and he still has big feet."

"He'll probably be tall like daddy."

Daniel's mom responded to the older children's remarks, "We noticed something about each of you as babies. Rebecca was very tiny, but ate so much and had lots of energy. Michael turned over in the hospital within a few hours of birth. He is still very strong."

They continued chatting about each person. Mom pulled out scrapbooks and baby books and they poured over the photos and notes.

What stories do you know about what your family noticed about you at birth? It's fun to share stories about someone's first days in the family whether an infant, or adopted at an older age. The New Year is also a great time to share stories of the past year and how members have changed. Take photos today to compare in the future.

Celebrate growth, learning, and what's unique about each person. Noticing and accepting each person's individual differences and changes is part of being a family.

God chose your family members. He accepts each family and wants to be your God. Choose to follow God as a family. Capture the memories of growing faith as a family with a journal that includes favorite stories, prayer answers, and scriptures.

Bible Story Connection 2 minutes

Focus on Jesus. Ask the children to act out the story of Jesus' birth as told in Luke 2:1-20. Read the story aloud as a family.

Chat Prompts: Options

● *"While Joseph and Mary were there, the time came for the child to be born. She gave birth to her first baby. It was a boy. She wrapped him in large strips of cloth. Then she placed him in a manger. That's because there was no guest room where they could stay."*

— Luke 2:6-7

Chat about your family's birth stories. Tell them about when you were born and when they were born.

MORE TIME?

● *"You are joined to Christ and belong to him. And Christ is joined to God."* – 1 Corinthians 3:23

Chat about being part of a much larger family—God's family. How do you see people serving God in your church? What are their talents that make them a good fit for that job? What talents do you have that can serve God as part of his larger family?

● *"Here is the written story of Adam's family line. When God created human beings, he made them to be like him."*

— Genesis 5:1

Chat about your extended family. Discuss being part of a larger legacy. Is there someone in the extended family that the children look or act like? Do you stay in touch with the extended family? Make a plan to connect to them this coming year.

Scrapbook/Prayer Journal Options

Add art that illustrates fresh starts and creation.

- Draw a rope or ribbon around the page to represent family ties. Add names on the ribbon of family members.

- Draw a family tree and add a few names from the past.

- Draw apples and note on them some of the qualities family members share.

Prayer

Father, thanks for inviting us to be part of your family. Help us know we belong to you and to our earthly family.

Wrap Up

Chat about what it means to belong to your family and to God's family. Have a group hug and express love for one another.

What's in a Name?

Family Beatitude: Happy is the family with a good name, for they will be respected.

Focus: Getting and keeping a good name and reputation.

Weekly Bible Verse: *"You should want a good name more than you want great riches. To be highly respected is better than having silver or gold."*

– Proverbs 22:1

Activity Options on a Good Name and Reputations

☐ Talk about how each person's name was chosen. Do a collage for each person that includes the reasons for his or her name and that person's good qualities, favorite dessert, snack, or main dish.

☐ Write some names of God on slips of paper, such as "Almighty," "Lord," and "Light of the World." Each day draw one name and chat about what it means. Type in Names of God in the search engine of your computer if you need help thinking of some.

☐ Fold a piece of paper and write a family member's name along the fold. Cut around the name and cut out the center of any O's and other letters with "open" centers. Open up the folded paper and see the artwork made from the name. Do this for each person. Hang them up or make a mobile with the cutouts.

The Important Thing About a Name 1-2 minutes

Karen's parents chose her name long before her birth; but they changed it when she was born. They'd planned to name her Noreen after her grandmother Nora. But on the day Karen came into the world, her mother said, "It's my Aunt Carrie's birthday. Let's name her Karen."

Many people have stories about their first names. One woman's parents had a long name in mind for their baby, but they changed it to Amy because it fit better since she was small. When they held the teeny little bundle, they chose a tiny, three-letter name.

God cares about each person's name. He renamed some people, including changing "Abram," which meant "noble father," to "Abraham," which meant "father of many." He knew Abraham's descendants would become a nation. Long before the birth of Jesus, God chose his name. It means "Deliverer" or "Savior."

The Bible tells us that what's more important than our names is making sure they are good, to be sure when people think of us, they think of good character traits such as honesty, kindness, and helpfulness. Family members help keep the family name good when they are known for their good deeds and character.

Bible Story Connection 2 minutes

Read Genesis 17:1-8 and 22:17-18 as a family. Pour a little sand or salt into each child's hand. Ask if they can count the grains. Talk about Abraham and why God renamed him.

Chat Prompts: Options

● *"You will become pregnant and give birth to a son. You must call him Jesus."* – Luke 1:31

Chat about the name "Jesus" and how God chose it before his Son's birth. Why does his name mean Savior?

MORE TIME?

● *"The gatekeeper opens the gate for him. The sheep listen to his voice. He calls his own sheep by name and leads them out."*
– John 10:3

Jesus described himself as the "Good Shepherd" (verse 11). He knows the name of each of his followers and cares for each one. God knows everything about you. How does that make you want to live?

● *"Do not be glad when the evil spirits obey you. Instead, be glad that your names are written in heaven."*
– Luke 10:20 NIV

The disciples obeyed Jesus and went ahead of him to places He wanted them to visit. They shared news about Him. When they returned to Jesus, they joyfully spoke of the good things that had happened and how spirits had obeyed them because of his name. Jesus replied that they should be joyful for a more important reason. He told them to rejoice because their names were written in heaven. Discuss what it means to have your names in God's book.

Scrapbook/Prayer Journal Options

Celebrate the names of people in your family by adding art to this week's scrapbook.

- Add each person's name written in that person's favorite color.

- Add words or designs that reflect the person's name and character.

- Add your family name with art that reflects what it means to you.

Prayer

Dear Father, thank you for caring about our names. We are grateful to have them in your book of life. Help us keep our names and reputations good.

Wrap Up

Discuss what each person did this week to help give his or her name a good reputation.

Affection

Family Beatitude: Happy is the family who shows affection, for they will feel loved.

Focus: Giving affection that expresses love

Weekly Bible Verse: *"[Mary] gave birth to her first baby. It was a boy. She wrapped him in large strips of cloth. Then she placed him in a manger. That's because there was no guest room where they could stay."*

– Luke 2:7

Activity Options on Affection

☐ Hold a time to snuggle this week. Gather together, get close, and read a book or tell stories.

☐ Be sure to hug one another each day. Add kisses or pats on the back.

☐ Take a walk together. Hold hands or link arms. Have an outdoor picnic if the weather is warm enough or an indoor picnic if it's cold outside.

☐ When family members walk in the door, greet them with smiles, hugs, and sweet words. Rejoice at being together.

Now I Feel Loved 1 minute

Rebecca climbed onto her parent's bed and wiggled her way between her daddy and mommy under the fluffy quilt. She hugged her daddy and then hugged her mommy. Then she said, "Now I feel loved!"

Hugs and cuddles, and even pats on the back, are signs of affection that help us feel loved. Whether we are with our mommy or daddy. We all want to be loved and to know we are lovable. It's good for mothers and fathers to be affectionate with their children and to show their love with positive words and hugs.

When Mary gave birth to her Son Jesus, she took tender care to wrap Him in warm cloths and gently place him in a soft bed of sweet-smelling hay. She wanted him to be warm and cozy. Other signs of affection include hugs, snuggling or cuddling together, pats on the back, and holding hands. Affection can also be shown by by acts of kindness and helping one another. Look for ways you each are showing love to each other this week. Be sure to point it out and tell them you feel loved when they do it.

Bible Story Connection 1 minute

Read aloud about Mary caring for Jesus in Luke 2:7. Now wrap each child in a hug and take extra time at night to tuck each one into bed.

Chat Prompts: Options

● *"So [the son] got up and went to his father. While the son was still a long way off, his father saw him. He was filled with tender love for his son. He ran to him. He threw his arms around him and kissed him."* – Luke 15:20

The son in this story ran away from home, spent his money foolishly, and wasted his time. He didn't stay home and help his dad like his brother did. When the son came home, instead of yelling at him, his dad ran to him and welcomed him. He was happy to see him. He forgave his son. Chat about forgiving one another. Discuss how we can still love someone even when they choose to do wrong things.

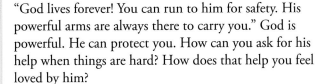

● *"Then he took the children in his arms. He placed his hands on them to bless them."* – Mark 10:16

Jesus showed love to the children by hugging them and blessing them (praying for them). Jesus loves your children. Talk about how it feels to know Jesus loves you.

● *"Love one another deeply. Honor others more than yourselves."* – Romans 12:10

"God lives forever! You can run to him for safety. His powerful arms are always there to carry you." God is powerful. He can protect you. How can you ask for his help when things are hard? How does that help you feel loved by him?

Scrapbook/Prayer Journal Options

Display art that shows affection in your family.

- Add kisses and notes that express love.

- Draw a suitcase and write what it's like to miss someone.

- Draw people holding hands and write about doing things together as a family.

Prayer

Dear Father, thank you for our family and the love we have for one another.
Help us live together in peace and show our love daily.

Wrap Up

Chat about what new ideas your family came up with to express affection.

Who Is God?

Family Beatitude: Happy is the family who believes in God, for they will know him.

Focus: Knowing God

Weekly Bible Verse: *"The Berean Jews were very glad to receive Paul's message. They studied the Scriptures carefully every day. They wanted to see if what Paul said was true. So they were more noble than the Thessalonian Jews."*

– Acts 17:11

Activity Options on Knowing God

☐ Read a verse that gives a name for God. Let the children draw what it means to them.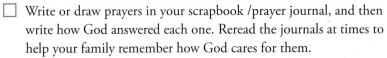
- Genesis 1:1, Creator
- 2 Samuel 22:3, Rock
- Psalm 23:1, Shepherd
- Hebrews 13:6, Helper

☐ Write or draw prayers in your scrapbook /prayer journal, and then write how God answered each one. Reread the journals at times to help your family remember how God cares for them.

☐ Take a "creation walk" or drive. Look at what God made and praise Him for His creativity.

☐ Read a Bible story and then act it out as a family. Chat about what the story teaches about God.

I Want to Know 1 minute

Becky said, "I want to go to Bible school with the big kids."

Mom said, "You're too young. Next year you'll be old enough."

Becky said, "But they are learning about God, and I want to know more about God too."

Her mother promised to talk with the Bible school teacher.

The teacher asked her mom to bring Becky to meet her.

After talking with Becky, the teacher said to Becky's mom, "She has a great love for Jesus. I think she'll be okay if you will stay with her in class."

Becky jumped up and down. "Hooray! I can go. I will be so good."

All week Becky woke up early and raced to the car when it was time to leave. She listened well and enjoyed all the activities. She retold the stories she learned to her dolls and her daddy when he came home each evening.

It's great to want to know God more and to be excited when you read the Bible and listen to Bible stories. God wants you to be excited about him. That's how you show you love him. It's also how you learn more about him.

Bible Story Connection 2-3 minutes

Read Psalm 136:1-9 and 23-26 out loud together. Each verse starts with something about God followed by: "His faithful love continues forever." Let the children echo that line after a parent or older child reads the first line of each verse. Add visuals and movement. For example, hold up images of the sun and moon or create arm motions for parting the Red Sea.

Chat Prompts: Options

Jesus said, *"You study the Scriptures carefully. You study them because you think they will give you eternal life. The Scriptures you study are a witness about me."* – John 5:39

What is a "witness"? Jesus spoke about reasons people study the Bible. What did the Psalm 136:1-9 tell us about God? Jesus told us the best reason to know the Bible—it tells us about God!

MORE TIME?

"I want to know Christ better. Yes, I want to know the power that raised him from the dead. I want to join him in his sufferings. I want to become like him by sharing in his death."
– Philippians 3:10

Paul preached about Jesus for a long time before he wrote these words. He knew a lot about Jesus, but Paul wanted to know him better. We can spend our entire lives learning more about God. We get to know him more as we follow him and talk to him and listen to him. As a family, talk about what you already know about God and why you want to discover more.

"[Wisdom calls out,] I love those who love me. Those who look for me find me." – Proverbs 8:17

God tells us that people who search for wisdom will find him. He wants us to get to know him. Talk about how God wants a relationship with each of us and wants us to talk to him. Ask what ways we can search for God, talk to him and hear him.

Scrapbook/Prayer Journal Options

Add art about what you and your family know about God.

- Write and draw about God. Draw and decorate a number 1 because God is the one and only God. Draw a big heart because God loves everyone. Draw big hands holding a globe because God made the world.

- Draw what you know about Jesus. Draw a cross with a heart on it because he loves you so much that he died for you.

- Draw an eye to remember to look around and see God's designs in his creation.

Prayer

Dear Lord, thank you for giving us the Bible so we can learn about you.

Wrap Up

Discuss what you learned about God this week.

Praise and Encouragement

Family Beatitude: Happy is the family who gives true praise, for they will be confident in God's love.

Focus: Praising and encouraging one another

Weekly Bible Verse: *"Build one another up every day. Do it as long as there is still time. Then none of you will become stubborn. You won't be fooled by sin's tricks."* – Hebrews 3:13

Activity Options on Praise and Encouragement

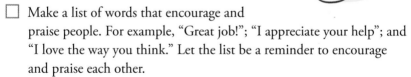

☐ At a meal, take time to encourage one another. Let each person describe noticing another family member working hard or learning a new skill. Applaud the family member and the encourager.

☐ Make a list of words that encourage and praise people. For example, "Great job!"; "I appreciate your help"; and "I love the way you think." Let the list be a reminder to encourage and praise each other.

☐ Discuss one skill each person is learning or improving. Encourage family members to help if they've already mastered the skill or to pray for each need they have. Later in the week, chat about how each person is progressing on his or her skill. Give more encouragement if needed. Take photos of them using their skills.

Learning Is Not a Race 2 minutes

"James, will you read to me?" Amber asked her big brother.

"You're learning to read, so why don't we sit together and we can each read our own books?"

"James, you have a big book. I might finish first."

"That's okay. Reading isn't a race. It's for fun and learning."

James and Amber sat beside each other on the couch and read. James eventually closed his book, and Amber looked up.

"Wow! You read that big book fast. I'm still working on my little book."

James smiled. "Thanks. I've been reading it a lot longer than you. When you're my age, you'll read faster. You're almost done with your book. Why don't you read the next page out loud to me?"

Amber grinned and read the page to her brother.

James said, "That's very good. I remember when you were just learning your letters and making the sounds for each one. You've learned a lot."

Amber smiled and nodded. "You're a great brother."

"Thanks. It helps me when you cheer me on. That encourages me."

Isn't it great when brothers and sisters encourage each other? Part of being a big brother or sister is helping teach younger brothers and sisters. Older siblings can be guides and coaches. All brothers and sisters can be cheerleaders who praise and encourage each other.

Bible Story Connection 1-2 minutes

Read 2 Corinthians 13:11. God calls us to make an effort at all times to encourage each other. This leads to a peaceful life. This is not easy for us. This verse tells us that God gives us love and peace. Talk about how we do our part to create a peaceful family. How does God help us?

Chat Prompts: Options

● *"Let another person praise you, and not your own mouth. Let an outsider praise you, and not your own lips."* – Proverbs 27:2

Chat about the difference between praise and bragging. Why does it sound better when someone else says good things about you?

MORE TIME?

● *"Encourage one another with the hope you have. Build each other up. In fact, that's what you are doing."*

– 1 Thessalonians 5:11

Chat about how encouragement helps people keep trying. Talk about things that each person finds hard to learn, whether riding a bicycle, learning a math skill, or putting together furniture. Discuss how encouragement builds up people.

● *"But build one another up every day. Do it as long as there is still time. Then none of you will become stubborn. You won't be fooled by sin's tricks."* – Hebrews 3:13

The Bible verse for this week teaches how important it is for us to help each other. When we build each other up we are encouraging the good in someone. Be on the watch for when you see family starting to make bad decisions. What are some ways you can lovingly let someone know they are making a mistake? What are some encouraging (building) words you can use?

Scrapbook/Prayer Journal Options

Add art that illustrates fresh starts and creation.

 Add artwork to your book to show how praise and encouragement are great building tools.

 Add stars with notes of praise about family members.

 Add big stars with praises for God.

Prayer

Dear Father, you are the Master Builder. Help us build up each other with words. Help us do right so we will be worthy of praise.

Wrap Up

Chat about who encouraged you this week. Discuss how well-deserved praise made you feel.

Faith: Talking to God?

Family Beatitude: Happy is the family who prays together, for God will hear them.

Focus: Prayer

Weekly Bible Verse: *"Where two or three people gather in my name, I am there with them."* – Matthew 18:20

Activity Options on Prayer

☐ Start family prayer time. Encourage family members to add prayers and praises to the family prayer journal.

☐ Make "praise cups." Decorate plastic cups with stickers or draw designs with markers. Cut slips of paper and let children write or draw about answers to prayer and praises they have for God. They can keep their praise cups near their beds and pull out slips to praise God in the morning or evening.

☐ Teach children this five-finger prayer:
  • The thumb is closest to them, so that's to pray for people in their family and their close friends.
  • The pointer finger is to pray for people who teach, guide, and help them (teachers, police, doctors).
  • The middle finger is tall, so pray for leaders and even the people your parents work for.
  • The ring finger is the weakest finger, so let that be a reminder to pray for anyone who is sick.
  • The baby finger is a reminder to be humble and pray for your needs last.

Prayer Time 1-2 minutes

"Time for prayer! Bring your prayer journals," Jim called.

When the family gathered together, they read over past prayer needs and noted answered prayers. Then, one at a time, each person stated one prayer need and one praise.

Jamie said, "I need prayer for remembering to practice my cello. I'm thankful for my good test scores."

Daniel said, "I need prayer to have less headaches. I praise God for my friends."

They all wrote notes in their journals. Prayers included help for upcoming tests, the need for a job, and some decisions about participating in ministries at church. Praises included making it to state on the swim team, the eldest child getting into college, and the gift of a toy airport.

The family held hands and started what they called their family prayer time. Each person prayed for the person to his or her left. They said a one-sentence prayer for a need and a one-sentence prayer for a praise.

Prayer Journal

They gently squeezed the hand of the next person as a signal it was that person's turn. The praying went full circle. The last person closed the prayer and said, "Amen."

They held a family prayer time every week and noted how God answered many prayers.

Bible Story Connection 1-2 minutes

Read what's known as the Lord's Prayer (Luke 11:1-4). Give each child a piece of bread to hold. Talk about basic needs and some of the basics of prayer. This prayer includes praise to God, a request to God to meet our needs, a request for God to forgive us, and a request to God to help us avoid sin.

Chat Prompts: Options

● *"One day Jesus was praying in a certain place. When he finished, one of his disciples spoke to him. 'Lord,' he said, 'teach us to pray, just as John taught his disciples.'"* – Luke 11:1

In response, Jesus taught what we now call the Lord's Prayer. Say the prayer aloud together and talk about the parts of the prayer. It includes greeting God, praising God, asking for forgiveness, requesting daily bread, protecting you from evil, and helping you trust God more.

MORE TIME?

● *"Give a lot of time and effort to prayer. Always be watchful and thankful."* – Colossians 4:2

Chat about taking time to really talk to God. "Being watchful" also means "to observe." Notice answers and blessings as well as praying about your problems. Be thankful.

● *"Here is what we can be sure of when we come to God in prayer. If we ask anything in keeping with what he wants, he hears us."* – 1 John 5:14

Chat about being faithful in prayer and the need to pray daily. Emphasize God's promise to listen and respond. Now read verse 15. Talk about how prayer gives you hope and how you feel knowing he listens to you.

Scrapbook/Prayer Journal Options

Add art to illustrate your prayer life.

- Draw praying hands, and write prayers on the fingers.

- Write the words of the Lord's Prayer and draw pictures to show what the words mean.

- Draw a crown for God's coming kingdom, bread for daily bread, and a heart for forgiveness.

Prayer

Our Father, you are Almighty. We thank you for our blessings and for forgiving our sins. Please care for our needs and help us follow you more closely. We commit our family to you. We promise to follow you.

Wrap Up

Chat about prayer and what you've learned about praying and God.

Hearing God

Family Beatitude: Happy is the family who listens to God, for they will stay close to him.

Focus: Hearing God

Weekly Bible Verse: *"If any of you needs wisdom, you should ask God for it. He will give it to you. God gives freely to everyone and doesn't find fault."* – James 1:5

Activity Options on Hearing God

☐ Take a walk at sunrise or sunset and share how God is painting a picture in the sky. Nature is his artwork to show us beauty.

☐ Listen to a Christian song or read from the Bible. Chat about what God said. Is there anything in the lyrics or Bible reading related to prayer? If so, write the words down and post them where everyone will see them daily.

☐ Be on the alert for when your children respond to God's word. Notice your children following God's rules, such as being kind. Mention that you saw your child living out what God teaches us in the Bible. Praise him or her for listening to God and following Him.

A Helpful Verse 2 minutes

Daniel tried to stay calm and not get angry when anyone teased him, but he often yelled, kicked, or punched when someone hurt his feelings. His family gave him ideas to help him remain calm, and they prayed with him. But he still had a hard time. He tried to think of jokes instead of the words being said. He tried to keep a little cross in his pocket to remember Jesus would help him stay calm. He still got angry and reacted.

One night he couldn't sleep. He woke up and paced around his room and prayed. Then he picked up his Bible and asked God for help. He opened the Bible to the book of Romans and started to read. When he came to Romans 6:12, he knew that God wanted him to remember that verse: "Don't let sin rule your body, which is going to die. Don't obey its evil desires."

Daniel thought about that and decided he didn't want to let sin be in control. He didn't want to give in to evil. He memorized that Bible verse. From that day on, when he started to get too angry, he remembered the verse and chose to not give in to evil. He thanked God for his help. Daniel was glad he was listening to God. He told his mother about the verse and how God answered his prayer. God listens to us. His words found in the Bible give us answers that help us:

"If any of you needs wisdom, you should ask God for it. He will give it to you. God gives freely to everyone and doesn't find fault." - James 1:5

If you think God has given you a good idea, write it down and chat about it as a family. If you choose to work on the idea, see what happens. As you discover what ideas work out when you pray, you'll be learning God's voice. Write about it in your prayer journal or this book.

Bible Story Connection **2 minutes**

Read 1 Samuel 3. Have the children lie down and close their eyes. Very softly whisper a name of one child. If the child hears his or her name, let him or her stand up. Do this for each child as a listening opportunity.

Chat Prompts: Options

"The Lord is ready to help all those who call out to him. He helps those who really mean it when they call out to him."

– Psalm 145:18

Chat about how to trust that God will answer prayer. He will respond. We need to listen and notice what happens, so we can know when God is answering.

MORE TIME?

"Don't worry about anything. No matter what happens, tell God about everything. Ask and pray, and give thanks to him. Then God's peace will watch over your hearts and your minds. He will do this because you belong to Christ Jesus. God's peace can never be completely understood." – Philippians 4:6-7

Encourage children to talk to God about everything. Talk about how God's answers bring peace. Encourage them to wait to feel peace about a decision or problem they pray about before taking action.

"When you do ask for something, you don't receive it. That's because you ask for the wrong reason. You want to spend your money on your sinful pleasures." – James 4:3

Chat about prayers that might be selfish, such as asking for a million dollars to spend on toys and games. Discuss God's will and what we should ask God.

Scrapbook/Prayer Journal Options

Add art to show you are listening to God.

- Draw ears and write down Bible verses and other ways God speaks to you.

- Draw a light bulb for the ideas God gives you. Write down those ideas.

Prayer

Lord, we are thankful that you listen to our prayers. Help us hear you.

Wrap Up
Discuss what everyone learned about listening to God this week. Talk about how prayer is an adventure that will last your entire lives.

Personalities

Family Beatitude: Happy is the family who accepts each person's uniqueness, for they will learn to live in harmony.

Focus: Understanding your unique personalities

Weekly Bible Verse: *"Christ has accepted you. So accept one another in order to bring praise to God."* – Romans 15:7

Activity Options on Personalities

☐ Look at pictures of the animals mentioned, or use stuffed animals, or make up your own animals to use. Chat about how each family member is like one of the characters. Discuss how that helps you understand one another.

☐ Plan a family activity and assign tasks according to the children's personalities. Kangaroos can plan the fun or be cheerleaders. Hyenas can work on details. Lions can schedule activities and lead some of them. Turtles can help plan the food jokes to go with the event.

☐ Add personality notes to baby books or scrapbook pages of each family member. Add the appropriate animal character. Let the page celebrate individual uniquenesses.

Bouncers, Bosses, and Bashful Babes 1-2 minutes

"I'm telling Mom. You can't tell me what to do."

"Stop bouncing on my blocks."

Sounds of bedlam filled the house. With four children of different personalities, this happened too often. They could easily be compared to animals people are familiar with. Michael bounced like a kangaroo, and Becky bossed others like a lion does. Darlene whined like a hyena until everything was perfect, and James usually remained calm like a turtle and sat at the table eating.

Mom gathered them together. They sat and listened to a story Mom made up about a kangaroo, lion, hyena, and turtle. The family chatted about the characters, and how each one acted like one of the funny characters. They all had good qualities, and yet they also had problems at times getting along because they were different. The kangaroo needed to remember that not everyone wanted someone bouncing around them, and the lion needed to know that not everyone wanted to be bossed.

Everyone talked about using his or her strengths to do something everyone could enjoy, like having a dance party. Turtle could plan the snacks. Lion could choose some music and make a plan for when to do each party activity. Kangaroo could plan games and a bouncy parade. And Hyena could set up a nice spot for anyone who wanted to sit and watch. This way everyone could have fun.

They shared how they could spend time together without fighting or hurting someone's feelings.

Gradually the whining and fighting changed a bit to happier phrases: "You are such a kangaroo, so bounce away where there's room to bounce." Or, "Remember, I'm like Hyena, so I want to take my time to make it perfect."

Bible Story Connection 1-2 minutes

Read about Jacob and Esau in Genesis 25:24-27. The boys were twins but had different interests and personalities. Hold up items that represent an interest of each child in your family. Talk about how everyone is different and unique.

Chat Prompts: Options

● *"How you [Lord] made me is amazing and wonderful. I praise you for that. What you have done is wonderful. I know that very well."* – Psalm 139:14

Talk about how unique personality traits help make your family special. Discuss how each member's strengths contribute to the family as a whole. How might a person's personality help him or her choose a career or make decisions? Thank God for each person.

MORE TIME?

● *"Lord, you have seen what is in my heart. You know all about me…God, see what is in my heart. Know what is there. Test me. Know what I'm thinking."* – Psalm 139:1,23

God understands each person and his or her personality. Chat about how understanding each person helps you get along better. What's something new you learned about a family member this week that helps you better understand that person?

● *"Because of God's grace I am what I am. And his grace was not wasted on me. No, I have worked harder than all the other apostles. But I didn't do the work. God's grace was with me."*
– 1 Corinthians 15:10

Paul used himself as an example. He wrote about how Christ used him even though he considered himself the least of the apostles. He accepted himself the way God made him and thanked God for his grace that gave him the ability to do great things. Chat about ways God can use each person with his or her personality and character traits.

Scrapbook/Prayer Journal Options

Celebrate personalities with illustrations and art.

- Draw animal characters and write names of family members who resemble the various traits.

- Draw the family activity you did this week, and write what each person did.

- Add positive words and art that describe family members.

Prayer

Father, thanks for making each person unique. Help us use our strengths and work on our weaknesses.

Wrap Up

Chat about what you learned regarding the people in your family. How will that help you get along better?

T-I-M-E Spells Love

Family Beatitude: Happy is the family who invests time in one another, for they will feel accepted.

Focus: Investing time in each other

Weekly Bible Verse: *"Make the most of every opportunity. The days are evil."* – Ephesians 5:16

Activity Options for Spending Time Together

☐ Plan family mealtimes as a "no electronic zone." Focus on listening and looking at one another. Discuss the day and add in other topics, perhaps using the Chat Prompts: Options from this book. Include Jesus by having a bread plate for bread or crackers. Jesus is the Bread of Life and is always present with you.

☐ Make a bread plate. Buy a solid-colored plastic plate and use permanent markers to draw bread or symbols for Jesus. Add a Bible verse if you'd like.

☐ Plan a family game night, or movie night, or family sharing memories night.

Look at Me! 2 minutes

George came to Daniel's home for dinner. The phone rang, but no one jumped up to get it. George looked around puzzled.

Daniel said, "It's our family mealtime, so we don't answer the phone. This is our time to be together."

Daniel's mom smiled. "The machine will take the message. We'll return the call later."

Daniel's family filled the mealtime with talk about the day and upcoming plans. They looked at one another, laughed, and shared. After the meal, everyone helped clear the table and do dishes.

It's good to spend time together and pay attention to each other—with electronics and phones turned off. In today's world, too often technology becomes more important than being present with real people. Have you noticed when walking in a park that it's not unusual to hear children yelling to their parents, "Look at me"? Unfortunately, the parents often are staring at their phones and clicking the keys to message someone. They're ignoring their little ones. As children grow up, they get phones too. They tend to copy their parents by spending their time online.

Online it's easy to find photos and comic strips of families together or visiting grandparents, except everyone is staring at an electronic gadget and no one is looking or speaking to each other. Instead, get refreshed with live conversations. Choose to turn off gadgets and phones for meaningful family time.

Bible Story Connection **2 minutes**

Discover how Jesus took time away from crowds to focus on his friends. Read Mark 6:30-31. Lead your children in a short parade to a quiet spot indoors or outside where you can be together. Talk about focusing on each other and supporting each other.

Chat Prompts: Options

● *"Teach us to realize how short our lives are. Then our hearts will become wise."* – Psalm 90:12

Chat about ways people waste time. How can you use time more wisely? How can you better schedule family time? What would be useful family time? Why is it good to have time to play and relax together?

MORE TIME?

● *"Children are a gift from the Lord. They are a reward from him."* – Psalm 127:3

Do you hide favorite gifts and never use them? That's not likely. Children are gifts from God. He wants parents to be excited about spending time with their children. Chat about the joy you felt when each child became a member of your family. Talk about the delight of spending time with each individual. Make plans to do more one-on-one activities.

● *"Make sure your children learn [God's commands]. Talk about them when you are at home. Talk about them when you walk along the road. Speak about them when you go to bed. And speak about them when you get up."* – Deuteronomy 6:7

God is part of your family, and he wants you to spend family time with him. Chat about some of the commands and blessings from God. When should you share about God? Always! Also talk about what each person likes about family devotions.

Scrapbook/Prayer Journal Options

Add art to this book to remember the time you spent together this week.

- Draw a clock and write the times of day you spent together this week.

- Draw your dinner table, and add food you enjoy eating together.

- Draw or add a photo of a fun family time.

Prayer

Father, help us spend time together as a family and include you. Help us talk about you every day.

Wrap Up

Schedule a time for another family activity. Chat about how God is part of your everyday lives and discuss how you can remember to talk to Him.

Listen!

Family Beatitude: Happy is the family who learns to listen, for they will have open hearts.

Focus: Really listening to each other

Weekly Bible Verse: *"My dear brothers and sisters, pay attention to what I say. Everyone should be quick to listen. But they should be slow to speak. They should be slow to get angry."* – James 1:19

Activity Options on Listening

☐ Cram a tube with socks and then talk through it to someone. Now take out the socks and talk through the tube. The socks blocked much of the sound. How can we keep from blocking out what people are saying? Do we cram too much into our minds and let stuff distract us from what is important?

☐ Make a "talking stick." Decorate a stick and tie on ribbon streamers. Use it when you have a family meeting or when there's an argument. The person holding the stick is the only one who gets to speak. When a person is done speaking, the stick is passed to the next person. This helps everyone stop, listen, and have a turn to speak.

☐ Practice listening skills, such as facing the speaker, looking into the speaker's eyes, clearing your mind of other thoughts, and rephrasing the message to be sure the speaker is understood.

☐ Read a story aloud and then ask questions about it or ask a child to retell the story in his or her own words.

An Apple 1 minute

"I'm so full I can't eat another bite," Mom said. A few seconds later she added, "But what I really want is an apple."

Michael stood up, strolled to the large bowl of apples on a counter, grabbed the biggest and reddest one, and handed it to his mother.

His mom stared at the apple for a few minutes.

Finally Michael's dad said, "Honey, you said what you really wanted was an apple."

Mom laughed. "I was looking at that bowl of apples, but what I meant to say was that I wanted a napkin. My mind picked up on the apples instead of my thought about a napkin. I didn't even listen to my own words!"

Everyone laughed while Michael got a few napkins for his mother.

Michael's mom admitted, "Sometimes I don't listen to what people say either. And sometimes I don't listen to God. I'd better clean out my ears and start paying more attention."

From then on, when Michael's mom didn't seem to be paying attention, instead of getting upset, someone would ask, "So, Mom, what you really want is an apple?"

She'd laugh and then turn to look at the person speaking. She'd really listen and pay attention with her eyes, her ears, and her heart.

Bible Story Connection 2 minutes

Read the parable of the soils in Luke 8:5-15. Point out that the disciples listened to Jesus and then asked him a question. Pass out seeds to the children. Ask if they can identify the plant from the seed. Let them know we don't always have all the answers, and neither did the friends of Jesus. Chat about how sometimes we may hear something and not understand it. Then we can ask questions like the disciples asked Jesus to get understanding.

Chat Prompts: Options

● *"My sons, listen to me. Don't turn away from what I say."*

– Proverbs 5:7

These words are a reminder to listen to our parents. Chat about a time a child didn't listen and obey. What happened? Why is it important to listen to wise words from a parent or authority figure, such as a teacher? Share when words from your parents helped you.

MORE TIME?

● *"The hearts of these people have become stubborn. They can barely hear with their ears. They have closed their eyes. Otherwise they might see with their eyes. They might hear with their ears. They might understand with their hearts. They might turn to the Lord, and then he would heal them."*

– Matthew 13:15

Jesus spoke these words based on Isaiah 6:9-10 to his close followers after he'd told a parable to a large crowd. He spoke about how people don't really pay attention or listen so they fail to understand. What can you do to listen better?

Scrapbook/Prayer Journal Options

Add art to illustrate good listening skills.

- Draw eyes and ears to remember to look and listen when someone speaks.

- Draw a stop sign to remember to stop and listen. Draw a yield sign to remember to give others a chance to talk.

- Draw a talking stick to remember that conversation includes talking *and* listening.

Prayer

Lord, help us really listen to one another and to you. Help us understand what we hear and to respond well. We want to know you and your Word so we'll have your wisdom.

Wrap Up

Chat about what you learned about listening better this week. How will you listen more attentively from now on?

Adventures in Learning

Family Beatitude: Happy is the family who likes learning, for they will become wise.

Focus: Learning new skills

Weekly Bible Verse: *"The Lord has filled him with the Spirit of God. He has filled him with wisdom, with understanding, with knowledge and with all kinds of skill."* – Exodus 35:31

Activity Options on Learning New Skills

☐ Try a new skill. Learn to make or do something, such as cooking or riding a bicycle. Take photos as each person tries a new activity. Add the photos to the scrapbook.

☐ Teach a household skill to children, such as doing the laundry, cooking, or pulling weeds. Show them how to do it, and then do the task alongside them. Take photos or record them as they work.

☐ Music skills are great to learn. Work on rhythm using sticks and pot lids. Encourage practice. For children who show interest and a willingness to practice, consider music lessons.

☐ Reward hard work. Celebrate practicing and improving by creating certificates or letting them choose an outing or reward.

FAMILY DEVOTION
• READ ALOUD •

Something New 2 minutes

Joseph opened his new building set and started following directions to put the model together. His brother, Thomas, wanted to help, so Joseph showed him how to look at the diagram and find the needed pieces to hand to him. Joseph said, "Thomas, this will help you learn about building and how to match the pieces to the pictures."

Meanwhile, their sisters Elizabeth and Lydia spent time with their mom learning how to sew. They had bought fabric for Elizabeth to make a curtain for her lower berth of the bunk bed. She only needed to sew straight lines. They needed to measure, fold the edges, and pin them to create hems. Elizabeth got tired of pinning, so her mother let her read while Lydia finished.

Then their mother showed them how to gently push the fabric under the pressure foot on the sewing machine to feed it through. She showed them how to tap the foot pedal to make the needle go up and down to form stitches. They practiced with paper and no thread in the needle first. Elizabeth, the oldest, worked the machine first while her mother worked the pedal. After a while, Elizabeth tried pressing the pedal. She worked at making the lines of stitches straight. Then Lydia took a turn. Soon they finished making the curtain and hung it up.

At the end of the day, the children showed the new building model and the new curtain to their dad. They smiled when he said, "Great job! You all learned new skills."

Long ago, God asked his people to build a special container called "the Ark of the Covenant" to hold the Ten Commandments (Exodus 25:10-22). God gave people the talent to work with wood, carve, shape metal, engrave, and more—every ability needed to make it. Remember, skills learned now can be used throughout life to share about God and his kingdom.

Bible Story Connection 2 minutes

In Exodus 31, read about the tent of meeting and other items God wanted his people to build. These were to be used as signs and reminders to follow God. God uses our skills to do the things he needs done on the earth. Talk about each of your skills. How can you use that talent for God.

Chat Prompts: Options

"The Lord has filled Bezalel and Oholiab with skill to do all kinds of work. They can carve things and make patterns. They can sew skillfully with blue, purple and bright red yarn and on fine linen. They use thread to make beautiful cloth. Both of them have the skill to work in all kinds of crafts." – Exodus 35:35

Natural talents to work with your hands, sing, and run fast come from God. List talents you've noticed in each person, and discuss good ways to use them. Let each person state one skill he or she wants to learn and set goals to help accomplish it.

"For the entrance to the tent the workers made a curtain. They made it out of blue, purple and bright red yarn and finely twisted linen. A person who sewed skillfully made it."

– Exodus 36:37

Becoming skilled at something takes practice. Ask each child what gifts they each have and how they can you get better at it.

"Stay excited about your faith as you serve the Lord."

– Romans 12:11

This verse encourages enthusiasm about God. How can you stay excited about your faith? How does being excited about your faith make it easier to talk about God?

Scrapbook/Prayer Journal Options

Add art that reflects the talents of each family member.

- Draw symbols for people's talents, such as needle and thread for sewing, tools or Lego blocks for building, and musical notes for singing.

- Draw or trace someone's hand and write notes of that person's talents on it.

- Draw smiles for enthusiasm and appreciating the talents of others.

Prayer

Creator God, thanks for giving each of us talents. Help us use them to serve you and the people around us.

Wrap Up

Celebrate everyone's talents with a show-and-tell evening.

Treasuring Easter

Family Beatitude: Happy is the family who believes in Jesus, for they will know love.

Focus: Understanding why Jesus died and the joy of Easter

Weekly Bible Verse: *"Gather for yourselves riches in heaven. There, moths and rats do not destroy them. There, thieves do not break in and steal them."* – Matthew 6:20

Activity Options for Celebrating Jesus

☐ Enjoy a treasure hunt like in this week's story or a traditional Easter egg hunt. Hide plastic eggs with Scriptures and treats inside. Here are a few verses to consider using: Proverbs 22:1; Ephesians 1:7; 3:8.

☐ Have communion as a family and chat about what we now call "the Last Supper." Wash one another's feet, praise Jesus, and break bread together. The Last Supper is described in four of the gospels (Matthew 26:26-28; Mark 14:22-24; Luke 22:19-20; John 13:1-17).

☐ Make or use store-bought cookie dough. Completely surround marshmallows with the dough and bake as directed. While the cookies cool, read about the empty tomb in John 1:1-18. When the children eat the cookies, they'll be amazed to find they're empty too.

Treasure Hunting 1-2 minutes

After church on Easter, everyone in the family sat down and waited for the treasure hunt to begin. Each person received a paper with his or her first clue.

Mom said, "The choice is up to you. You can forget the clue and not look for a treasure or you can accept the challenge and follow the clues. That's like the offer of eternal life from Jesus. You can choose to follow Jesus or you can choose not to follow Him."

The children chorused, "*Wahoo!* We'll follow Jesus. We'll follow the clues too." They took off, finding and unscrambling more codes, looking up Scripture verses, and figuring out the location of the little treasures that would lead to the big one. Younger children had easy jigsaw puzzles to put together that showed where to look.

Everyone met back in the family room and displayed their treasures.

Mom said, "It looks like everyone is happy today. Do you know there are greater reasons to rejoice than finding presents?"

The children nodded. One said, "Jesus died for us, and then he rose from the dead. He came back to life."

"Yes!" Mom said. "He loves each one of us. When we break a rule, we have to make things right. When people sinned, it caused a break with God. When Jesus died, he made things right again. Because Jesus died for us, God forgives our sins when we tell him we are sorry."

One of the children said, "I'm happy that he came back to life. That's an awesome reason to celebrate!"

Bible Story Connection 2-3 minutes

Read Luke 23:33-46. Tell your children what this means to you.
How did you come to know Jesus? How did you feel when you
realized he had died for you?

Chat Prompts: Options

● *"Jesus is not here! He has risen! Remember how he told you he would
rise. It was while he was still with you in Galilee. He said, 'The Son
of Man must be handed over to sinful people. He must be nailed to
a cross. On the third day he will rise from the dead.'" 8 Then
the women remembered Jesus' words."* — Luke 24:6-8

Have each person write out or dictate a thank you letter/prayer
to Jesus for dying on the cross for us. Add it to your scrapbook/
prayer journal.

MORE TIME?

● *"Mary kept all these things like a secret treasure in her heart.
She thought about them over and over."* — Luke 2:19

Chat about how we need to do more than memorize
scripture and read it. We need to think about it. What
scriptures do you think about again and again?

● *"Jesus said to her, 'I am the resurrection and the life. Anyone
who believes in me will live, even if they die.'"* — John 11:25

Jesus said these words *before* he died. He knew he would
be crucified, and he also knew he would come back to life.
Jesus knew he would die for you. He loved you that much.
How does that make you feel?

Scrapbook/Prayer Journal Options

Add symbols of Jesus and his resurrection to your book to illustrate your faith in him and eternal life.

- Add a cross or nails and write about how much Jesus loves you.

- Add an empty tomb and flowers and write about the joy of Jesus's resurrection.

- Draw a treasure chest and write about real treasure that lasts.

Prayer

Lord, thank you for dying for us. We are happy you rose and opened the gates of heaven. We are thankful we will live with you always.

Wrap Up

Discuss what you know about the death and resurrection of Jesus. Chat about what is really valuable.

Understanding

Family Beatitude: Happy is the family who works to understand each other, for they will show mercy.

Focus: Understanding one another

Weekly Bible Verse: *"Finally, I want all of you to agree with one another. Be understanding. Love one another. Be kind and tender. Be humble."* – 1 Peter 3:8

Activity Options on Understanding

☐ Ahead of time, remove batteries from a flashlight. Then ask someone to get the flashlight and turn it on. When it doesn't work, ask them to figure out the problem. Discuss how it helps to investigate when there's a problem so a person can understand how to fix it.

☐ Watch the clouds together and see what happens to the weather. That's "listening with your eyes." Talk about how science helps us understand how nature works. Jesus spoke about that: "Jesus…said, 'You see a cloud rising in the west. Right away you say, "It's going to rain." And it does' " (Luke 12:54).

☐ Make a railroad crossing sign to remember to stop, look, and listen to one another to help you understand actions and words. Decorate the sign with eyes and ears and hang it up. Practice good listening skills, including paying attention and responding.

☐ Let people "walk in the shoes" of other family members. Point out that some shoes will be too small and some will be too big. Discuss what it means to understand another person's perspective.

Lights Off! 1-2 minutes

Michael yelled, "Hey, who turned off the lights?" He groped in the dark for the light switch and flipped it on.

Hmm. It seems that someone likes to sneak around and turn off lights on people, Michael's mom decided. She'd keep an eye on the light switches. Only one of her children hadn't had a light problem lately.

A day or so later, she caught James. He'd tiptoed near the door and was about to flip the switch when his mom grabbed his hand. She gently held him and walked him into her room. "James, I want to know why you keep turning off the lights on everyone."

He didn't say anything.

"James, are you upset with Michael and your sisters?"

He nodded.

"When you are upset, you can talk to your daddy or to me. What happened that upset you?"

Slowly James explained that Michael had taken one of his toys without asking, and his sisters hadn't let him play a game with them. He didn't like to argue, so he'd decided to play tricks on them with the lights.

Mom called everyone together and announced she'd caught the "light" culprit and discovered a few problems. The children listened to how they'd hurt James's feelings and how James had decided to bother them in return. Everyone apologized and decided they should be more considerate. James agreed to speak up when he felt left out or hurt.

Bible Story Connection **2 minutes**

Read Acts 9:36-43. Peter takes time to understand the friends of
Dorcas, who had died. Peter cleared the room and then prayed. God
answered, and Dorcas was brought back to life and healed! Peter
listened to his friends and cared about them. He wanted to help them.
Listening shows caring and helps us understand each other. Practice
each telling a story and using good listening and caring skills.

Chat Prompts: Options

● *"By wisdom a house is built. Through understanding it is made
secure."* – Proverbs 24:3

Chat about how taking time to understand each family member
builds a stronger family. What can you do to be more
understanding? How does knowing that people care enough to
understand you make you feel more secure?

MORE TIME?

● *"I want all of you to agree with one another. Be
understanding. Love one another. Be kind and tender. Be
humble."* – 1 Peter 3:8

God wants us to live in harmony. How does understanding
help maintain harmony? What does it mean to be humble?
When members of your family disagree or fight, how can
you help each other resolve it? Create a disagreement action
plan. How do you disagree, listen, and resolve conflicts?

● *"If you really want to become wise, you must begin by
having respect for the Lord. All those who follow his rules have
good understanding. People should praise him forever."*
– Psalm 111:10

What have you learned from the Bible this week? How does
following God's rules give you more understanding? What
rules do you need to work on following better?

Scrapbook/Prayer Journal Options

Add art to represent your improved understanding.

- Add hearts with eyes on them to remember to look, listen, and understand with your heart.

- Add chain links all around the page to recall that understanding helps everyone stay connected.

- Draw a Bible to remember that following God gives you wisdom and understanding.

Prayer

Lord, give us understanding hearts. Help us to listen and notice the needs of one another. Help us understand the feelings of each family member.

Wrap Up

Discuss what you've learned about each other this week that has deepened your understanding of your family.

Approval

> **Family Beatitude:** Happy is the family who applauds accomplishments, for they will feel approved.
>
> **Focus:** Showing approval
>
> **Weekly Bible Verse:** *"Jesus became wiser and stronger. He also became more and more pleasing to God and to people."* – Luke 2:52

Activity Options on Approval

☐ Use stamps or stickers as rewards to show your approval when a child does a job well. Consider having a family notebook for the stickers. Write down the name of the child, the chore, and let the child paste in the sticker. Review the book often as a family.

☐ Make lists of chores for each child to learn basic household tasks. Rotate the jobs. Place stars on a child's chore list for effort and mastery. Think about new tasks that will help your children gain more skills and knowledge.

☐ Create a treasure box. Inside, place slips of paper with rewards, such as a hug, a special walk, 15 minutes extra time before bed, a day off from a chore. Use these as rewards to show your approval.

☐ Use a thumbs-up or other "family known" sign of approval when someone does something helpful or finishes a task.

Glow Rings 1-2 minutes

The house was filled with the clatter of dishes, a broom swishing back and forth, and children humming. Lydia and her siblings quickly finished up after-dinner chores and started to get ready for bed. Then the sound of water running and a timer buzzing signaled the children taking turns brushing their teeth for two minutes each. They ran into the family room and announced, "We're ready for bed."

"Great! I smell nice, clean breath. Let's see who did their chores." Mom and Dad walked through the house. They spotted a clean table, beds made, and toys picked up. "Wow! We have some great workers. That gives us happy hearts. We have a surprise for everyone because you did your work."

Mom handed out glow rings. The children slipped them on their fingers and jumped up and down, yelling, "Oh yeah!"

Dad read from the Bible about Jesus growing and pleasing God, the Father. Jesus obeyed his parents. Mom and Dad praised their kids and tucked them into their beds. Everyone turned on their rings, and Mom and Dad said a prayer. Soft pink, blue, green, and yellow light glowed under the blankets.

Bible Story Connection **2 minutes**

Read Hebrews 11:23-28. This chapter is often called "the hall of faith." God approved of the faith in Moses. This whole chapter shows many people who showed their faith in God. Start your own hall or board of faith. Set up a space where you can post notes and pictures of family members accomplishing something that reveals they trust God and follow Him. Post reminders that God approves of their love and faith.

Chat Prompts: Options

● *"His master replied, 'You have done well, good and faithful slave! You have been faithful with a few things. I will put you in charge of many things. Come and share your master's happiness!' "*
– Matthew 25:21

A master said these words when he returned from a trip and found out how two of his workers had wisely used their talents to increase his profits. He rewarded their efforts. What can you work to improve? What are great phrases that show approval? Make a list and use those phrases this week.

MORE TIME?

● *"Do not work for food that spoils. Work for food that lasts forever. That is the food the Son of Man will give you. For God the Father has put his seal of approval on him."* – John 6:27

Jesus spoke to them about heaven and their need for him, the Bread of Life. He said that people who come to him would not be hungry. He was talking about *spiritual* hunger. What will we have forever if Jesus is our Lord and Savior?

● *"Do your best to please God. Be a worker who doesn't need to be ashamed. Teach the message of truth correctly."*
– 2 Timothy 2:15

God wants us to seek his approval first. Sometimes people expect you to do something that isn't right. They will approve of you if you do the wrong thing. Should you care about their approval? Talk about a time this happened to each of you.

Scrapbook/Prayer Journal Options

Add symbols and art that shows giving and receiving approval.

- Draw smiles and write what God wants for your success.

- Draw bread or rolls and words about food that lasts.

- Add stickers and stars to reflect giving and receiving approval.

Prayer

Lord, help us obey you and follow your guidance, including obeying parents and other authorities. Thank you for approving our efforts to know you better.

Wrap Up

Talk about what each person has accomplished in the past week, including the effort put in toward reaching goals. Discuss how it feels to receive approval.

Hope

Family Beatitude: Happy is the family who keeps hoping for the best, for they will stay positive.

Focus: Hope

Weekly Bible Verse: *"When you hope, be joyful. When you suffer, be patient. When you pray, be faithful."* – Romans 12:12

Activity Options on Hope

☐ Look at your wall calendar. Add activities to do in the future. Chat about looking forward to those fun times. That's creating hope.

☐ Take a walk on a sunny day. Notice how flowers turn toward the sun. Sunflowers turn to the sun that helps them grow. When we turn to God or a person for help, we have hope. Make a paper sunflower as a reminder to keep hoping.

☐ Write down goals for each person. Talk about the hope of reaching the goals, and explore the steps needed to realize success. Encourage each person to work toward his or her goals. Remind them that you believe they can reach for the stars and succeed.

☐ Make a large paper cross. On it have everyone write about his or her hope in God. Hang it up where the family can see it often.

☐ Make a little hope chest. Decorate a box, and fill it with Bible verses on hope and positive words. Keep it where family members can pull out a slip of paper and read a message when they want or need encouragement.

"I Can Do It!" 1-2 minutes

Elizabeth complained, "I'm so bad at basketball. I can't even win in a one-on-one competition against a little boy."

"He's the coach's son, and he's fast and strong. You're improving, and that's what's important. You still can't shoot the ball high enough to get it in yet, but you're getting closer. Maybe you can keep him from getting one in and cause a tie."

"I can try that. I need to run fast and block him."

Elizabeth prayed for strength. She worked hard all week by practicing good blocks against her older brother.

At the next one-on-one, she walked onto the court with a smile and the hope that she would meet her goal. Her older brother yelled, "Go, Elizabeth! You can do it."

Her opponent kept trying to dodge and go around her. Elizabeth stayed between him and the hoop. Once in a while, she knocked the ball out of his hand and grabbed it. She'd dribble toward the other hoop until her opponent would snatch the ball away. Elizabeth twirled her body, ran down the court, and blocked him again and again. At last the whistle blew. She wiped sweat off her forehead. She heard her brother yell, "You did it, Elizabeth! Wow!" No one had scored. A tie—just like she'd hoped for.

Her coach said, "Great blocking. That's the way to go. I hope you'll keep working hard."

Bible Story Connection 1-2 minutes

Read 1 Corinthians 9:24-27, which is about running a race. What helps a person keep running to the end? Set up a race course and run to the finish line.

Chat Prompts: Options

"That's how we should live as we wait for the blessed hope God has given us. We are waiting for Jesus Christ to appear in his glory. He is our great God and Savior." – Titus 2:13

What is the biggest hope this verse talks about?

MORE TIME?

"Appoint Joshua as the new leader. Help him to be brave. Give him hope and strength. He will take these people across the Jordan. You will see the land. But he will lead them into it to take it as their own." – Deuteronomy 3:28

God spoke these words to Moses. He wanted Moses to train Joshua to be a leader. That included giving Joshua hope for the future. How can you give people hope? How do your parents give you hope?

"This is why we work and try so hard. It's because we have put our hope in the living God. He is the Savior of all people. Most of all, he is the Savior of those who believe."

– 1 Timothy 4:10

These words were written to teachers who helped people grow in faith. How are your parents doing that? Why is it important that parents teach you about God? What difference does hope in God make in your life? How does knowing God believes in you help you keep going?

77

Scrapbook/Prayer Journal Options

Add art to reflect the hope you have.

- Add a cross with words of your hope in Jesus.

- Draw a hope chest with words of encouragement on it.

- Write a math problem someone in the family learned to solve.

Prayer

Father, we are thankful for the hope we have in you. Help us live with hope each day.

Wrap Up

Discuss your hopes for the future.

Success

Family Beatitude: Happy is the family who strives to meet goals, for they will be successful.

Focus: The measure of success

Weekly Bible Verse: *"All hard work pays off. But if all you do is talk, you will be poor."* – Proverbs 14:23

Activity Options on Success

☐ Use a timer to check the speed of each family member in running or doing a task. Discuss ways to improve. Practice the activity during the week, and then time everyone again to see the amount of improvement. Improvement shows success for hard work.

☐ Play games with targets. Toss balls into a bucket or hang up a bull's-eye and try to hit it with a ball. Try it blindfolded and note how it's easier when you can see and aim for the target. Use this as an opportunity to talk about setting realistic goals.

☐ Cut out two large paper hearts. Write the two greatest commandments on them from Matthew 22:37-40. Write words or draw pictures that show how to follow these rules. Chat about how this will bring success.

☐ Schedule time for each person to work toward personal goals, homework, and other skills. Evaluate the progress and decide if the time set aside is enough.

Success at Last! 2 minutes

Five-year-old Rebecca dove into the pool for her first race. The tiny girl, much younger than the other swimmers, stretched one arm out at a time as she fluttered her feet up and down. She moved slowly, way behind the other swimmers.

As the racers climbed out, they looked back to see Rebecca about halfway across the pool. One teammate shouted, "Go, Becky! Go, Becky!"

All the parents of their team also started chanting, "Go, Becky!"

Rebecca kept stroking. She made it three-quarters across the pool, her yellow swim cap bobbing side-to-side with each breath she took.

Then the swimmers on the other team who had finished joined in the cheering, followed by everyone in the stands. The crowd stood and applauded when Rebecca's hand touched the side of the pool. She climbed out almost five minutes after the other swimmers. She waved to the people who were still clapping, thanking them for their encouragement.

It took all Rebecca's strength to make it the length of the pool that day. She continued swimming and worked hard to get a little faster each time she dove in.

Years later, Rebecca served as co-captain of her high school swim team. She worked as a lifeguard at the community pool during summers and taught children to swim. She never forgot her first meet and the joy of touching the wall when she finished. She remembers being cheered on that day—and she always cheers on her teammates and students.

Bible Story Connection 1-5 minutes

1 Kings 6 tells about all the detail of King Solomon building the temple. Read verses 37-38. It took him 7 years to build the temple. If you have more time, read through all of 1 Kings 6 and see how much detail he added. Take a walk around your home and talk about how it was built and the time needed to keep it looking nice.

Chat Prompts: Options

- *"Commit to the Lord everything you do. Then he will make your plans succeed."* – Proverbs 16:3

  How can you commit your plans to God? What plans have you made to help you reach a goal? What other steps can you add to the plan? Have you prayed about your goal?

MORE TIME?

- *"Never stop reading this Book of the Law. Day and night you must think about what it says. Make sure you do everything written in it. Then things will go well with you. And you will have great success."* – Joshua 1:8

  How will God's Word help you be successful? How is God's measure of success different from the world's?

- The apostle Paul wrote, *"I do not run like someone who doesn't run toward the finish line. I do not fight like a boxer who hits nothing but air. No, I train my body and bring it under control. Then after I have preached to others, I myself will not break the rules. If I did break them, I would fail to win the prize."* – 1 Corinthians 9:26-27

  Discuss running tips. What helps a person run faster? Is it hard to run with your eyes closed or not looking forward? What does God want you to focus on? How do you stay focused on various goals?

Scrapbook/Prayer Journal Options

Add art to celebrate family and individual successes.

- Draw trophies with the names of each person who has worked hard.

- Draw a sneaker and eyes, along with words on keeping your eyes on your goal.

- Draw some blue ribbons, stars, and other symbols for success. Add family names and the ways they succeeded this week.

Prayer

Thank you, Lord, for blessing us with talents. Help us work hard to use our talents and succeed. Thank you also for the wonderful hope and goal of being with you in heaven.

Wrap Up

Discuss what it means to succeed. Chat about who has worked hard this week and how it helped improve a skill.

Trust

Family Beatitude: Happy is the family who trusts one another, for they will grow strong together.

Focus: Trust

Weekly Bible Verse: *"When Peter saw the wind, he was afraid. He began to sink. He cried out, 'Lord! Save me!'"* – Matthew 14:30

Activity Options on Trust

☐ Go for a swim if there's an indoor pool nearby. In the bathtub, practice breathing for swimming.

☐ Check to see what toys and items float and what ones sink. Talk about how water can hold things up.

☐ See if you can find a bird learning to fly or a baby learning to walk. It takes trust for a bird to leave the nest and for a baby to get up and move when he or she keeps falling down.

☐ Set up an obstacle course. Have one person be blindfolded and another person responsible for leading or talking that person through the course. Take turns doing each role. Talk about the trust needed to succeed.

Trust Me 2 minutes

"No, Mommy! Don't let go! I'll drown." Lydia flailed in the water and clung to her mother's arm.

"Lydia, it's okay. I'll hold you. Then, as you start to float, I'll drop one hand a little lower. I can catch you if I need to. I'll be right here."

"No, Mommy! Don't let go. Keep your hand on my belly."

"Lydia, stand up." Mommy lifted her daughter upright to show her she could stand in the shallow water.

Lydia looked around and sank down a little as her face turned pink. "Well, as long as we stay right here, I'll try to float."

"Stand here for a minute and watch me float." Lydia's mother lay on her face and floated. Then she flipped over, stretched her arms out wide, and floated on her back.

When it was Lydia's turn, the girl still shook with fear and yelled for her mom to hold on tight.

"Lydia, you always trust me when you jump to me from the stairs. You can trust me now. I love you so much that I would never let you get hurt while you learn to float."

It took many tries and a few days in the pool for Lydia to trust her mother and discover she really could relax and float.

Trust issues around water are not new. Peter, a fisherman, practically lived on the water. He fearlessly stepped out of the boat when Jesus said, "Come." But when the disciple felt the wind, he panicked and started to sink. Like Lydia, he cried out for help. Jesus reached out and saved him.

Something about water—the flowing or the lightness—makes it hard to trust it will hold us. Parents want to do what's best for their children, even in water. God also wants what's best for us.

Bible Story Connection 2-3 minutes

Read about Noah trusting God (Genesis 6:13-22; 9:11-17). Noah had never seen rain or a flood, but he trusted God and built the ark. God protected Noah, his family, and each type of animal. Go outside and use the hose to shower everyone with water. Let the children use umbrellas as protection.

Chat Prompts: Options

● *"[The Lord] commanded our people who lived before us to teach his laws to their children...Then they would put their trust in God. They would not forget what he had done. They would obey his commands."*
– Psalm 78:5,7

This psalm recounts God's care for Jacob and his people, the Israelites. It also reminded them how often they disobeyed. When they disobeyed God, he let their enemies capture them. But still he cared for his people and eventually restored them. What has God done for you in the past? How can knowing what God has already done help you trust God in the future?

MORE TIME?

● *"Suppose you can be trusted with something very little. Then you can also be trusted with something very large. But suppose you are not honest with something very little. Then you will also not be honest with something very large."* – Luke 16:10

Trust often comes or is given a little at a time. You need to work at being trustworthy every day. What can you do to show you can be trusted?

● *"Let all those who go to you for safety be glad. Let them always sing for joy. Spread your cover over them and keep them safe. Then those who love you will be glad because of you."*
– Psalm 5:11

Talk about the safety of your home and how your children can trust you to help keep them safe.

85

Scrapbook/Prayer Journal Options

Illustrate your trust in God and in each other with symbols and words.

- Draw a key and talk about how family members guard your home and hearts.

- Draw about a time God cared for you and showed you that you can trust him.

- Draw a bird learning to fly.

Prayer

Father, thank you for caring for us every day. Help us obey you and trust you in everything.

Wrap Up

Chat about what you learned about the importance of trust this week. Discuss how to be more trustworthy.

Overcoming Fears

Family Beatitude: Happy is the family who calms fears, for they will be courageous.

Focus: Overcoming fear

Weekly Bible Verse: *"Do not be afraid. I am with you. Do not be terrified. I am your God. I will make you strong and help you. I will hold you safe in my hands. I always do what is right."* – Isaiah 41:10

Activity Options on Fear

☐ Try some optical illusions. Hold your pointer fingers a short distance apart, at eye-level, and slowly bring them closer to your eyes until you see a piece of your finger floating. Eyesight can trick us.

☐ Memorize a scripture that will help you feel brave, such as Joshua 1:9, where God says to have courage and promises to be with you. Tuck a small object, such as a cross or stuffed animal, into your bed at night as a reminder that God is with you.

☐ Check out bugs and other creepy crawlers together. Learning facts about creatures and other objects a child might fear will help a child overcome fear.

The Nightmare 1-2 minutes

"D-d-d-d-a-d-d-y, I'm s-s-s-c-a-r-e-d!" Liam cried as he shivered.

"Did you have a bad dream?"

"Yes! A monster chased me, and I couldn't get away."

"Well, there's no monster with you. Let's go look in your room."

Liam hopped onto his dad's back so he could stay close and Dad would enter the room first.

They shone a flashlight in every direction. They saw nothing but dirty, smelly clothes and a few toy cars scattered on the floor.

Daddy tucked Liam into bed and sat with him for a little while. He said a prayer and turned on the nightlight. Once Liam started breathing slowly and drifting off to sleep, Dad tiptoed out of the room.

Everyone dreams, and sometimes a scary dream can seem very real. A few grownups in the Bible talked about dreams that scared them. King Nebuchadnezzar couldn't sleep when a dream bothered him. He wanted help, but he wanted to test his wise men by not telling them the details. They couldn't figure it out. Only Daniel trusted the one true God and prayed for his help. God showed Daniel the dream and its meaning. In sharing what God showed him, Daniel calmed the king's fears.

Bible Story Connection 1-2 minutes

Read how the disciples shook with fear in Luke 24:37-43. What were they afraid of? Jesus calmed their fears by showing them his hands and feet and eating food to prove he was alive. Use a flashlight and cast shadows on the wall with objects to help you talk about fear.

Chat Prompts: Options

● *"While Pilate was sitting on the judge's seat, his wife sent him this message. It said, 'Don't have anything to do with that man. He is not guilty. I have suffered a great deal in a dream today because of him.'"* – Matthew 27:19

Chat about dreams and nightmares. Discuss how even powerful and famous people have nightmares. Talk about what helps a person feel calm and brave.

MORE TIME?

● *"Here is what I am commanding you to do. Be strong and brave. Do not be afraid. Do not lose hope. I am the Lord your God. I will be with you everywhere you go."* – Joshua 1:9

God spoke these words to Joshua, the leader of the Israelites after Moses. God knew Joshua and his army would face many enemies and fight many battles. He reminded Joshua to be brave and that he would be with him. God also knows your future, and he wants you to be brave and trust him. Talk about times you were afraid and then felt brave and overcame your fear.

● *"Turn all your worries over to him. He cares about you."*
– 1 Peter 5:7

Let each person share a worry or fear. When everyone is done, pray about each person's worry. Ask God to take care of each one. Talk about what might help each person fear less.

Scrapbook/Prayer Journal Options

Add art as reminders of ways you can be brave.

- Add optical illusions and drawings of eyes as a reminder to check unknown things out before getting scared.

- Draw a mask and write about how hidden things can be scary.

- Draw a hand as a reminder that you are not alone. You have a family who loves you and a God who loves you and protects you.

Prayer

Father, help us be brave. Help us remember that you love us and are always with us.

Wrap Up

Discuss how family members faced some fears this week and what helped them trust God and find peace.

Fresh Starts

> **Family Beatitude:** Happy is the family who knows that forgiveness allows a fresh start, for they will know relief.
>
> **Focus:** Fresh starts
>
> **Weekly Bible Verse:** *"Lord, have mercy on us. We long for you to help us. Make us strong every morning. Save us when we're in trouble."*
> – Isaiah 33:2

Activity Options on Starting Over

☐ Take a walk and look for signs of new life. Examine plant buds, fresh grass, baby birds, and caterpillars. God gives the Earth a new start every spring. Seasons are another reminder of fresh starts.

☐ Wash clothes together. Talk about how the water and soap washes away the dirt and smells to give clothes a fresh look and clean scent. Another fresh start!

☐ Watch a sunrise together. Talk about how the new day dawns and God paints a new picture in the sky as light overcomes darkness.

☐ Plant a seed. Chat about how it is placed in the dark soil all alone. With water and nutrients from the soil, the seed sprouts and finds the sun. The plant grows. Each day is an opportunity to do something new and start something again.

Let's Start the Day Over

2 minutes

Freddie screamed. His face turned red. He dropped to the floor and kicked his feet and flailed his arms in a huge tantrum.

His mother had trouble calming him down. Her efforts seemed to make him worse. She was sympathetic because she knew Freddie struggled with keeping his blood sugar even. That meant his energy and mood levels went up and down a lot. Maintaining a good blood-sugar level was like trying to balance on a seesaw. If he had too little sugar in his blood, it was like sitting on the end of a seesaw that landed with a thud. Too much sugar and he was barely hanging on as the seesaw flipped him up.

Freddie didn't like losing control and screaming. He was just hurting inside. He was glad his mom understood what was happening. She'd say, "Let's just start the day over. Erase what went before and try again." Then they'd hug, and Freddie's teary face would smile with relief. "Yes, let's start over!" he'd agree.

And they did. Love would rule the moment. The atmosphere would change, and they usually went on to have a happy day.

It's great when moms and dads understand the need for a new start. God understands that too. He gives us strength every morning for a new day. God says that when his people—and that includes you and me—make bad choices, he will give us a new heart and a new spirit.

Bible Story Connection **2 minutes**

Read about Saul (renamed Paul) in Acts 9:1-22. Take turns blindfolding family members and having them try to identify objects. Talk about how God blinding Saul for a time allowed him to see the truth and gave him a fresh start as a follower of Jesus. When you were blindfolded, what was different?

Chat Prompts: Options

● *"Get rid of all the evil things you have done. Let me give you a new heart and a new spirit. Then you will be faithful to me. Why should you die, people of Israel?"* – Ezekiel 18:31

What old habits and bad choices do you want to get rid of today? What can you do to approach life in a new way…to restart? How can your family help you restart?

MORE TIME?

● *"We also have the message of the prophets. This message can be trusted completely. You must pay attention to it. The message is like a light shining in a dark place. It will shine until the day Jesus comes. Then the Morning Star will rise in your hearts."*
– 2 Peter 1:19

The Bible has a message about new life in heaven for everyone. Chat about how Jesus gives you a fresh start. What promises of God help you restart? What gives you hope that life will get better when you face problems and work through them?

● *"His great love is new every morning. LORD, how faithful you are!"* – Lamentations 3:23

Start each day with a word from God. Also start it with a good breakfast, encouraging words, and a hug. Chat about how each day is a new opportunity. How can each person encourage his or her family members as they work on new starts?

Scrapbook/Prayer Journal Options

Add artwork to reflect the idea of new starts.

- Draw soap and bubbles and write about clean starts.

- Draw a sunrise and write about new days.

- Draw an empty heart and fill it with words of love and encouragement.

Prayer

Dear Lord, thank you for loving us and giving us new days—a lifetime of new days. Thanks for forgiving us and allowing new starts.

Wrap Up

Talk about what new starts each person had this week. Does anyone want a fresh start right now?

Discipline

Family Beatitude: Happy is the family who disciplines their children, for they will be respectful.

Focus: Discipline

Weekly Bible Verse: *"No training seems pleasant at the time. In fact, it seems painful. But later on it produces a harvest of godliness and peace. It does this for those who have been trained by it."* – Hebrews 12:11

Activity Options on Discipline

☐ Make a picture chart for morning and bedtime routines. Give children a star for doing each activity. Explain that this is part of learning self-discipline.

☐ Make a behavior chart with rules, consequences, and rewards.

☐ Use a traffic signal system to help with discipline for a particular behavior problem. Start each day with a green dot. Switch to yellow as a warning if there's a problem. Post a red light if a child has disobeyed and will receive a consequence.

☐ Training and practice are part of being a disciplined person. Let a child choose a skill to learn or improve, such as running fast or playing an instrument. Set up a practice chart and add stickers for successful practices and measureable progress. Set a reward system for acquiring a set number of stickers.

FAMILY DEVOTION
READ ALOUD

Drive-by Kisses 1-2 minutes

Thomas peeked out from his door, blew kisses, and said, "I love you, Mommy. I love you, Daddy."

"Go to bed!" they replied together.

Thomas lay back down for a little while and then repeated blowing kisses.

His parents called this activity "Thomas's drive-by kisses." Every night they kissed Thomas and reminded him that they loved him but expected him to stay in bed and go to sleep. He needed to follow the rules. If he followed his bedtime rules, he would get a sticker in the morning.

Each morning after a night of blowing kisses, Thomas watched his mother pass out stickers to his brother and sisters. He'd say, "But I went to bed."

"But you disobeyed by not going to sleep."

"It was just to say I love you. That's good to do."

"It's good to do when you're allowed to be awake. When you break good rules, you aren't showing love."

One night, Mom stuck a glow-in-the-dark sticker where Thomas could see it from his bed. She said, "If you think about getting up, look at the sticker. Blow a kiss to the sticker and say, "I love you, God. I will obey my parents by staying in bed and going to sleep."

That helped Thomas remain in his bed. He grinned in the morning when his mother gave him a sticker.

Bible Story Connection **2 minutes**

Read about how Mary was worried about Jesus. Jesus in Luke 2:41-52.
Play the game of Hide-and-Seek. Talk about the fun of finding the
hidden person. Discuss how it's not fun when a person is really
missing and that children letting their parents know where they are
is part of being respectful.

Chat Prompts: Options

● *"Our parents trained us for a little while. They did what they thought
was best. But God trains us for our good. He does this so we may
share in his holiness."* – Hebrews 12:10

Discuss how rules keep you safe, help you improve, and make
home a better place. What are some rules in the home that show
parents do what they believe is best?

MORE TIME?

● *"Put up with hard times. God uses them to train you. He is
treating you as his children. What children are not trained by
their parents?"* – Hebrews 12:7

Chat about how practicing and following rules can be hard.
What are the rewards? Why do good parents train and
discipline their children?

● *"We have all had human fathers who trained us. We
respected them for it. How much more should we be trained by
the Father of spirits and live!"* – Hebrews 12:9

Talk about how much nicer it is at dinner and other times
when everyone behaves well and is polite. How does training
and discipline help? Chat about how God trains us.

Scrapbook/Prayer Journal Options

Add art to show what good discipline is and how it works.

- Add a musical instrument or sneaker as a symbol of training.

- Add the cross as a symbol of how Jesus died to fulfill God's plan.

- Draw a traffic sign and write a rule on it that you need more practice doing.

Prayer

Father, help us follow your rules, and practice our new skills. We are thankful for rules that will make us better people.

Wrap Up

Discuss the benefits of discipline and the choice to keep practicing new skills.

Summer Fun

Family Beatitude: Happy is the family who enjoys summer fun, for they will build memories.

Focus: Enjoying sunshine, stars, and God's Son

Weekly Bible Verse: *"You decided where the borders of the earth would be. You made both summer and winter."* – Psalm 74:17

Activity Options for Summer Fun

☐ Sleep out under the stars. Use an app or a chart of the summer sky to locate constellations.

☐ Enjoy water fun at a nearby waterway or in a pool. Make a water scope to investigate creatures or other items in the water. Use a plastic bucket or bottle. Cut off the bottom. Stretch a piece of clear plastic wrap across the bottom opening. Secure plastic tightly with tape or a rubber band. Push bottom into the water and look through the top opening. The view will be magnified.

☐ Grow a snack like cherry tomatoes, beans, or peanuts. Watch the stages from sprouting to ripening. Enjoy the results of your labor.

☐ Try new recipes with fresh produce. You could make kale chips by breaking kale into small pieces, sprinkling it with salt and seasonings, and roasting it in the oven. Bake and eat stuffed zucchini. (Scoop out seeds and fill hollow with mix of 6 crushed crackers, 2 teaspoons chopped nuts, and 1 tablespoon butter. Bake at 400 degrees for about 10 minutes until top browns.)

Lazy Days and Starry Nights
1-2 minutes

Jamie and his family hauled sleeping bags, pillows, and blankets to the backyard. They set up an area to sleep under the stars. In the moonlight, they checked the vegetable garden for some fresh snacks. They picked cherry tomatoes, green beans, and small cucumbers.

Jamie's dad built a small fire, and they toasted marshmallows. They sang some songs, including "On a Starry Night." The clear sky let them see many twinkling lights as they lay down and looked up.

Jamie pointed and said, "I see three stars in a row."

Dad said, "That's called Orion's belt." He then pointed out the big dipper, little dipper, and the North Star in the end of the little dipper's handle.

Mom read some Bible verses about the stars.

Jamie said, "I learned that stars are like the sun. They are big balls of fire. It takes a long time for their light to reach the earth."

Dad said, "That's true. God made such a huge universe that the distance from us to those stars is very far." Then he asked how they'd spent the hot day while he was at work.

Jamie said, "We played on the waterslide and used a bucket of water to paint secret pictures on the porch. They dried up so you can't see them now. Then we licked the ice pops we made yesterday until they disappeared."

Dad smiled. "It's nice to have a few lazy days in summer. I'm glad I can enjoy a relaxing night with you."

Bible Story Connection 1-2 minutes

Read Matthew 6:27-34. Jesus used flowers and birds to teach us not to worry. Pass out feathers or flowers. Let everyone examine these natural treasures. Talk about the fun of carefree summer days.

Chat Prompts: Options

● *"[God] made the Big Dipper and Orion. He created the Pleiades and the southern stars."* – Job 9:9 *"He made the moon and stars to rule over the night. His faithful love continues forever."* – Psalm 136:9

Check out the night sky during the summer. What constellations can you find and name? How does the beauty of God's creation reveal His love?

MORE TIME?

● *"You are the one and only Lord. You made the heavens. You made even the highest heavens. You created all the stars in the sky. You created the earth and everything on it. And you made the oceans and everything in them. You give life to everything. Every living being in heaven worships you."* – Nehemiah 9:6

God made a world filled with nature, which includes waterways, stars, and the earth itself. What are signs of life around you? What wonders are in the sky and under the water that you enjoy watching? What do you enjoy when you walk outside? Have you noticed any area that needs care? How can you help care for creation? How do creatures worship God or reveal the creativity of God?

● *"Learn a lesson from the fig tree. As soon as its twigs get tender and its leaves come out, you know that summer is near."*
– Mark 13:28

Summer fun includes growing plants and picking produce. Chat about the stages of a plant cycle and how they relate to the seasons God established. What do we see in nature that shows God's care for us? (Water/rain, sun/warms, trees/wood, plants/animals - food, etc).

101

Scrapbook/Prayer Journal Options

Use art to illustrate what you learned about nature this week.

- Draw stars and write down the names of constellations.

- Draw a plant you grew or a favorite fruit or vegetable. Write down what God supplies to help them grow.

- Draw an ant. Write down what wisdom you can learn by watching ants.

Prayer

*Father, thanks for the sunshine
and the fun of summer.
Thanks for the stars in the sky
that twinkle and shine.*

Wrap Up

Chat about the wonders of nature that you enjoy in the summertime. Plan another outdoor time of family fun.

Money Sense

Family Beatitude: Happy is the family who learns balance with money, for they will thrive.

Focus: Money attitudes

Weekly Bible Verse: *"Hands that don't want to work make you poor. But hands that work hard bring wealth to you."* – Proverbs 10:4

Activity Options to Develop Good Money Attitudes

☐ Make a chart of ways your children can earn money, such as doing extra chores.

☐ Go shopping to price the items the children want. Help the children set goals for getting something they want and start saving. Chart their progress.

☐ Play games that use play money to help children learn to handle money and think about how it is used.

☐ Use real money for teaching how to count and make change. Make sure children learn the value of each coin and bill.

Money-Making Stand 1-2 minutes

"Mommy, can we get ice cream and go to the movies today?"

The children had a new request every day of summer vacation that mostly involved their mom spending money.

"Kids, you need to do things that don't take money," Mom said. "Or you need to earn some money of your own."

The children decided to play games and make their own snacks.

Mom asked the children to help in the garden. She mentioned that they had too much zucchini and had already passed out a lot to their neighbors. They'd also baked bread and muffins.

Becky said, "Why don't we have a zucchini bread stand?"

Mom agreed, but she said they needed to make plans and use some money earned to cover the required ingredients, such as flour.

They checked the cost to make each loaf, made "Bake Sale" signs, and baked lots of bread. Then they started their business. They sold every loaf of bread! They added muffins, recipes, and fresh zucchini to the stand.

They paid Mom for the ingredients and divided the rest between themselves. After setting some aside to give at church, they still had money to spend.

Mom asked, "So, are you enjoying your vacation?"

They decided they'd spent so much time working that they weren't having fun. They chose to open the stand only two days a week. That gave them time for fun and time to earn money.

Bible Story Connection **2 minutes**

Read about Joseph's wisdom when running the finances and grain storage in Egypt in preparation for a coming famine (Genesis 41:46-57). His choices saved many people from starvation. He also had time to be a husband and dad.

Chat Prompts: Options

● *"Don't be controlled by love for money. Be happy with what you have. God has said, 'I will never leave you. I will never desert you.'"*
– Hebrews 13:5

How can you think the way God wants you to about money? What helps people make God and other people more important than money? How do people waste money? Discuss being content with what you have and using money wisely. For more on being content, read Philippians 4:12-13. What does the family want to spend money on this week?

● *"Love for money causes all kinds of evil. Some people want to get rich. They have wandered away from the faith. They have wounded themselves with many sorrows."* – 1 Timothy 6:10

Chat about how some people abuse money and hurt people to get money. Some people steal and others trick people. What can you do to be sure you handle money correctly?

● *"'Bring the entire tenth to the storerooms in my temples. Then there will be plenty of food. Test me this way,' says the Lord. 'Then you will see that I will throw open the windows of heaven. I will pour out so many blessings that you will not have enough room to store them.'"* – Malachi 3:10

Everything we have comes from God. In the Old Testament God asked his people to give him just one penny out of every ten cents. That is called a "tithe." Talk about giving to God. We can give our time not just our money. Ask how you can give one tenth of your money and time to God.

Scrapbook/Prayer Journal Options

Remember how to handle money wisely by adding art.

- Draw coins or bills and write about good money attitudes.

- Draw a piggy bank and name something you are saving to buy.

- Draw a church and write how much you plan to give to God.

Prayer

Father, thanks for blessing us with the ability to work and earn money to pay bills. Thank you for our home, food, and clothes. Help us use our money wisely.

Wrap Up

Talk about the best attitudes toward money and the wise money choices people made this week.

Life Skills

Family Beatitude: Happy is the family who learns life skills, for they will be competent.

Focus: Developing life skills

Weekly Bible Verse: *"My brothers and sisters, you were chosen to be free. But don't use your freedom as an excuse to live under the power of sin. Instead, serve one another in love."* – Galatians 5:13

Activity Options for Life Skills

☐ Cook and bake together. Make sure each family member can cook a meal. Keep ingredients on hand for what they can cook. Encourage each child to help prepare dinner once a week.

☐ Do laundry with children. Teach them to sort clothes, add detergent, use the washer and dryer, and fold clothes. Help them check for stains and use stain remover. Show them how to make simple repairs to clothes, such as sewing on a button or stitching up a seam.

☐ Help children learn to use basic tools, including a hammer, screwdriver, and pliers. Let them help put together new toys.

☐ Make outdoor garden care a family project. Rake, plant, water, and weed together. Help older children learn to mow the grass. Let each child choose a plant to add to the yard. They can care for what they plant. Teach them to weed.

I'll Help! 1-2 minutes

Maria tripped and landed with a thud. She winced with pain when she started to stand. She called, "Thomas, come help me!" Her five-year-old son spun around and came back. Maria reached out her hand. "I fell, and I need help getting up." Thomas took her hand and tugged. Maria got up and leaned on her son. They hobbled to a nearby bench.

Maria's older children found them a few minutes later after they'd finished basketball practice. Joseph, who was ten, helped his mom hop to the car. She drove home, gritting her teeth against the pain. Then Joseph helped her hop into the kitchen. He got ice to put on his mom's swollen ankle.

Joseph said, "Mom, if you have kielbasa, I can cook dinner. Grandma taught me."

Mom nodded.

Joseph checked and found all the ingredients. He chopped potatoes, broccoli, and the kielbasa. He started cooking them in separate pans. He asked his siblings to set the table and pour drinks.

Dad came in and said, "Smells good. Is that kielbasa and home fries?"

Maria said, "Yes. Joseph is cooking dinner. I hurt my ankle."

Dad gave Joseph a big hug and then looked at Maria's ankle. He got an ace bandage, wrapped her ankle, and gave her some medicine to help the swelling go down.

They ate dinner together, and then the older children washed the dishes and got the younger ones ready for bed.

Maria said, "You kids have been great today. I really needed your help. I might need help for a few more days."

The children were a huge help They pitched in. They washed and sorted clothes, cooked more meals, and cleaned the floors and bathrooms for the entire week.

Bible Story Connection 1-2 minutes

Read about a woman from Shunem, who cared for a prophet
(2 Kings 4:8-11). She and her husband built a room for him.
Discuss what she put in the room. He must have liked her hospitality
and cooking. What skills did she use?

Chat Prompts: Options

● *"God's gifts of grace come in many forms. Each of you has received
a gift in order to serve others. You should use it faithfully."*
– 1 Peter 4:10

God wants us to use our gifts. These include preaching, and
teaching, and service. Talk about what talents family members
have and how they can be used in your home.

MORE TIME?

● *"Carry one another's heavy loads. If you do, you will fulfill
the law of Christ."* – Galatians 6:2

Talk about how family members can use skills they learn to
pitch-in at home. What is each person best at? How can that
ability help in the house?

● *"She gets up while it is still night. She provides food for her
family. She also gives some to her female servants."*
– Proverbs 31:15

Discuss what Mom does and what "holes" need to be filled
when she is sick or hurt. What supplies should be on-hand
for children to make meals? How can each person in the
family help lighten her workload?

Scrapbook/Prayer Journal Options

Add art to reflect the life skills of family members.

- Draw favorite foods family members can cook.

- Draw clothes as a reminder to learn skills to care for clothing.

- Draw a few tools and the repairs or projects family members have used them on.

Prayer

Father, thanks for our family. Help us pull together, especially when someone is hurt. Help us be cheerful about pitching in when extra help is needed.

Wrap Up

Discuss what life skills family members have learned and how they can apply them. Enjoy a day of doing home repairs together or a day of cooking together.

Patriotism

Family Beatitude: Happy is the family who is patriotic, for they will value freedom.

Focus: Valuing freedom

Weekly Bible Verse: *"Blessed is the nation whose God is the Lord. Blessed are the people he chose to be his own."* – Psalm 33:12

Activity Options on Patriotism

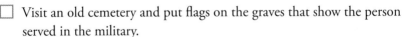

☐ Participate in a parade or watch one to celebrate American Independence Day on July fourth. Decorate your home with a flag and colors of the flag. Make a centerpiece to display our countries colors. Look at the Declaration of Independence, Constitution, and other documents of our country. Notice where God is mentioned.

☐ Visit an old cemetery and put flags on the graves that show the person served in the military.

☐ Make foods that use the colors of the flag, such as a strawberries and blueberries dessert with whipped cream. Discuss the meanings behind the colors (red for courage and bloodshed, white for purity, blue for the stars in the heavens and to represent justice).

Secret Tunnel 1-2 minutes

Rebecca wore red, white, and blue. She waved her American flag as she watched the parade. Her family listened and watched as bands played and marched. They looked at the floats pass by and snapped some photos. Then they headed for a family picnic at the home of Rebecca's great-great aunt.

Rebecca met some of her mother's cousins and their children. Her cousin Paul showed Rebecca his house. It was built in 1710 and included a secret tunnel. Rebecca watched as Paul lifted the door and peered into the narrow tunnel.

"Where does it go?" she asked.

Paul took her down a little way and said it went way out beyond the house.

"Why is there a tunnel?" Rebecca asked.

"When they built the house, they were afraid of Indians. They built the tunnel in case they needed to escape. It ended in the woods back in those days."

"Wow!"

"Later, the house owners hid slaves who were escaping their owners in the tunnel. It was part of what's called the "Underground Railroad."

"This house has a lot of history," Rebecca said.

"Yes. The early families fought in the American Revolution so we would have freedom."

"I have some ancestors who came over in the 1600s. They were in prison in England for their faith and found freedom to worship here."

Paul replied, "That's cool. I'm thankful our families helped found our country and that we have freedom. Hey, I smell burgers and hot dogs. Let's go eat!"

"Yes! And later we can watch fireworks. It's a great day."

Bible Story Connection 2 minutes

Read Exodus 3:7-10. God called Moses to be a leader and to free His people. God understood our need for freedom. Read how Moses responded to God in Exodus 4:10-17. God wants us to help people be free. How will you respond?

Chat Prompts: Options

● *"Christ has set us free to enjoy our freedom. So remain strong in the faith. Don't let the chains of slavery hold you again."* – Galatians 5:1

Christ died on the cross to pay the punishment for what we have done wrong. He has set us free. When we ask for forgiveness and believe in what he did, we are new people. We don't have to behave the same way anymore. God's power is now helping us be strong. How do you feel when you are forgiven instead of punished when you do something wrong?

MORE TIME?

● *"No one has greater love than the one who gives their life for their friends."* – John 15:13

Jesus spoke about his willingness to give his life so we would have eternal joy in heaven. Chat about what this means to you. Discuss the sacrifice that people in the military make to protect our freedom, including their willingness to die. Mention any family members who fought in wars, and pray for any who are serving now.

● *"All of you must obey those who rule over you. There are no authorities except the ones God has chosen. Those who now rule have been chosen by God."* – Romans 13:1

Discuss how authority comes from God. Talk about reasons to respect our leaders. Pray for leaders to choose to follow biblical principles and listen to God. Chat about how sometimes people protest laws they consider unfair or against their faith and how that fits in with Scripture.

Scrapbook/Prayer Journal Options

Use art to reflect your patriotism and how you honor your countries leaders and authorities.

- Draw a flag and write about a parade you've seen.

- Draw the outline of your state and write about ways to share your faith.

- Add splashes of your country's colors and fireworks to the page. Write a prayer for freedom of religion to continue.

Prayer

Father, thank you that we live in a country where we are free to worship you. Help us protect our freedoms and understand our government. As parents, guide us to vote wisely.

Wrap Up

Talk about patriotism and your citizenship in heaven. How can you show you care about freedom—especially freedom of religion?

Politeness

Family Beatitude: Happy is the family who is polite, for they will be pleasant.

Focus: Politeness and manners

Weekly Bible Verse: *"Tell them not to speak evil things against anyone. Remind them to live in peace. They must consider the needs of others. They must always be gentle toward everyone." * – Titus 3:2

Activity Options on Politeness

☐ Have your children host a lunch or get-together so they can practice good manners. Invite company and have them remember to welcome guests, use good manners, and enjoy polite conversation.

☐ Have a game night and be polite to winners and losers. Focus on having fun and laughing.

☐ Teach children how to set a table for a meal. Add some napkin folding to make it fun. Practice politely passing and serving food. Take turns praying over the food at meals.

☐ Make a welcome basket for company. Fill it with soap, toothbrushes, combs, and other items overnight guests might forget or need. Add a welcome note.

Welcome 1-2 minutes

Juliette, three years old, opened the door and greeted her mother's cousin Marie. "Hello. My mother will be right down. Please come in." She smiled and her brown eyes twinkled.

She showed their guest to the living room and asked if she would like to sit. She offered to get her a drink of water or iced tea. She bounced out of the room and returned carefully holding a full glass with two hands.

Once she handed Marie the glass of iced tea, Juliette asked if she wanted a cookie. She said she'd helped her mother make them. After bringing orange-cranberry cookies out on a plate, she sat and asked, "How are you doing?" She looked at Marie and listened to her reply.

Marie planned to stay for a few days. She responded to Juliette's questions. Every morning and evening, Juliette asked Marie how she was doing and if she needed anything. When Marie had free time, Juliette offered to play games and asked what one Marie liked. Juliette lost, but laughed and said they could choose another game. Juliette won this time and said, "You played very well."

While Marie visited, one of Juliette's friends came to play. Juliette greeted her friend warmly and took care of her. She let her choose the activities. She also introduced her friend to Marie.

Marie complimented her cousin on Juliette's manners and hospitality. Her cousin replied, "Juliette loves company. She's such a little lady."

116

Bible Story Connection **2 minutes**

Read about the hospitality and politeness of Abraham and Sarah in Genesis 18:1-8. Discuss the words Abraham used and what he did to make the guests feel welcomed. As a family, make welcome cards to give to your visitors.

Chat Prompts: Options

• *"[Jesus said,] 'Anyone who welcomes you welcomes me. And anyone who welcomes me welcomes the one who sent me.'"* – Matthew 10:40

Chat about welcoming someone as if you were welcoming Jesus. How would you feel if Jesus came to your house? What would you do or say differently?

MORE TIME?

• *"Welcome others into your homes without complaining."*
– 1 Peter 4:9

Why is this a good motto for how to treat company? How does this impact how you play games? Are you a good sport? What does that mean? Does it make a win feel better if the loser congratulates you? How can you help someone who loses feel better?

• *"[Jesus] turned toward the woman. He said to Simon, "Do you see this woman? I came into your house. You did not give me any water to wash my feet. But she wet my feet with her tears and wiped them with her hair."* – Luke 7:44

Think about how you've felt when you visited people who made you feel comfortable and when you visited people who didn't. What can you do to be sure your visitors feel welcome?

Scrapbook/Prayer Journal Options

Add welcome notes and art to your book.

- Draw a door and smiley faces. Write words that welcome people.

- Add an angel and note on how to treat visitors.

- Draw a game piece or mini game board and write notes on how to be a good sport.

Prayer

Father, we are thankful for our home. Help us welcome visitors and treat them as if we are serving you or your angels.

Wrap Up

Start at your front door and walk in as though you are a visitor. From the welcome mat on, what is there to make someone feel welcomed?

The Great Outdoors

Family Beatitude: Happy is the family who enjoys the great outdoors, for they will appreciate God's creation.

Focus: Appreciating nature

Weekly Bible Verse: *"Let the heavens be full of joy. Let the earth be glad. Let the ocean and everything in it roar."* – Psalm 96:11

Activity Options with Nature

☐ Take a walk and decide what activities are outside to try. Make a list of adventures to plan and enjoy as a family. Schedule one and prepare for it, gathering any needed supplies.

☐ Go on a picnic. Watch the clouds and look for items in the shapes. Check out the local foliage, rock formations, and other natural landscapes. Sketch them or take photos.

☐ Enjoy outdoor sports and try new ones. Take photos as you learn and master a sport. Cheer on family members who belong to a team in an outdoor sport.

☐ Make and fly a kite or windsock on a breezy day.

☐ Plan an activity to help care for God's creation. It might be pulling weeds, picking up litter, joining a team to clean a local waterway, or planting seeds or trees.

Wave Attack 1-2 minutes

The roaring waves crashed into Kyle, shoving him back to the shore. He sat up, giggled, and crawled toward the waves again. He splashed and tried to swim through them. At eighteen months, he was determined to attack and conquer the ocean. Later, Kyle took a cup and copied his mom in filling it with sand and dumping it out to make a castle. Then he stood up and stomped through the castle, sending sand flying everywhere.

After dinner, Kyle watched the sunset, pointed to the colors, and waved goodbye to the sun. He looked up and pointed toward the twinkling stars.

Kyle's mom laid him on his back on a blanket, and he fell asleep watching the night sky.

Toddlers have a natural joy for nature and a zest for life. Kyle started swimming as an infant and appeared fearless. Challenging waves and wind brought giggles. As he grew, Kyle liked hiking, camping, scuba diving, white-water rafting, horseback riding, rock climbing, tree climbing, and any other outdoor activity.

He also enjoyed animals, and they liked him. His cat became a fur wrap that stayed on him as he played and raced around the house. During his school years, Kyle preferred reading animal adventure stories to any other type of book.

God created a world full of joyful possibilities that Kyle relished.

Bible Story Connection 1-2 minutes

Read about waves in Mark 4:35-41. Talk about the storm and how Jesus reacted. Remember, he made the water in the sea that splashes on the shore.

Chat Prompts: Options

● *"Ever since the world was created it has been possible to see the qualities of God that are not seen. I'm talking about his eternal power and about the fact that he is God. Those things can be seen in what he has made. So people have no excuse for what they do."* – Romans 1:20

These words reinforce the knowledge given in the beginning of the Bible about creation. It is easy to examine creation to discover the Creator's existence. What do you see around you that tells you God created it? (Intricacies of flowers, the perfect distance from the sun, the seasons, how a body is designed, etc.)

MORE TIME?

● *"The earth belongs to the Lord. And so does everything in it. The world belongs to him. And so do all those who live in it."*
– Psalm 24:1

Chat about the wonders of nature. Let everyone mention favorite outdoor places, activities, flowers, and animals.

● *"Let the fields and everything in them be glad. Let all the trees in the forest sing for joy."* – Psalm 96:12

Look at the glorious and varied colors outdoors. Notice how even the dirt is in different colors and shades. Listen to the sounds of nature. Take a whiff and smell the plants, ocean, lakes, and other outdoor scents. Go outside and praise God for his creation.

Scrapbook/Prayer Journal Options

Let nature images and colors splash onto the book's pages.

- Draw plants that live in your area.

- Sketch creatures that live near you and the pets that live in your home.

- Draw a natural wonder you'd like to visit.

Prayer

Creator, thank you for making such an amazing world. Help us spend time outdoors discovering the beauty you made and enjoying the adventure it provides.

Wrap Up

Discuss what you can do to protect nature in your area and how you can enjoy the outdoors more.

Work Ethics

Family Beatitude: Happy is the family who puts their hearts into their work, for they will have good work ethics.

Focus: Work ethics

Weekly Bible Verse: *"Work at everything you do with all your heart. Work as if you were working for the Lord, not for human masters."*
– Colossians 3:23

Activity Options on Work Ethics

☐ Take your child to work and let him or her see you in action. Talk about your career and what you like about it.

☐ Chat about enjoying a nice home and how the work to keep it nice is a labor of love. Choose a job to do together to maintain the house or yard. Remind your children they are doing the work for Jesus too.

☐ Set up a system for your children to clean their rooms. This includes having a place where everything goes. Set up steps for cleanup, such as first making the bed, and then picking up the biggest toys. Do an inspection afterward and praise your children when they do a good job.

☐ Make chore time fun. Turn on music, work together, and talk about the importance of each job.

Ready for Company 1-2 minutes

"Sean, when I'm shopping, I'd like you to clean up the backyard. Remember, your cousins are coming to visit today, and we want everything to look nice."

"Okay, Mom."

A few hours later, Sean's mom returned. She saw Sean vacuuming the kitchen floor. "I smelled freshly cut grass. You must be tired from cleaning the yard. You even did the edging," She commented.

"I'm fine. I mowed, edged, and weeded too. I cut some roses and put

them on the table. I tracked in mud, so I started vacuuming the floor."

"Fantastic! You're building those muscles. You must be happy to have Steve coming to visit. I picked up your favorite ice cream to go with the cookies I made. You'll need an extra scoop tonight with all the calories you've burned today."

Sean's mom smelled the roses and smiled. "I hope Dad and your sister get home soon. Our guests should arrive anytime, and this is the first time they've visited us."

"It's a four-hour drive."

"I know. And we see them when we visit Grandma. Your uncle has business here this week."

Dad strolled in, and a blur of color raced past. "Rachel won her game! She's racing upstairs to change. And I noticed the lawn is mowed and trimmed. Great job, Sean." He rumpled Sean's hair. "You did more than I expected. Now I can relax with our company. Listen! I hear car doors slamming. Must be my sister and her family."

Bible Story Connection 2 minutes

Read about people working on rebuilding the wall around Jerusalem (Nehemiah 2:18; 3; 4:14-21). When enemies tried to stop them, they still worked. Talk about the last project/work your family did together. Was it easy, hard, fun, long, or short? How did each person contribute?

Chat Prompts: Options

● *"I also told them how my gracious God was helping me. And I told them what the king had said to me. They replied, 'Let's start rebuilding.' So they began that good work."* – Nehemiah 2:18

Nehemiah challenged the Israelites to work. They'd been afraid to rebuild Jerusalem's walls, and it lay in ruins for seventy years. The people had forgotten to trust God and started to believe the lies and teasing of their enemies. Nehemiah's pep talk got them to agree to work. They completed the work in fifty-two days. Chat about what inspires you to work. How should your children respond when someone teases and says they aren't capable of doing something?

MORE TIME?

● *"They must work. They must do something useful with their own hands. Then they will have something to give to people in need."* – Ephesians 4:28

Chat about how working brings money you can use to bless people. What can you do to help people by working hard? How will doing something useful with your hands make you feel?

● *"Work at everything you do with all your heart. Work as if you were working for the Lord, not for human matters."*
– Colossians 3:23

God wants us to remember when we have a task to do that we should do it as though we are doing it for him. How will this change how you do a job or chore?

Scrapbook/Prayer Journal Options

Decorate in your scrapbook to celebrate your hard work.

- Draw hands and write notes about working.

- Draw coins for money earned, and write about generous ways to use money.

- Draw pictures of chores each person does to help at home. Surround the pictures with hearts as reminders to work with all your heart.

Prayer

Father, thanks for giving us hands and legs that help us work hard. Bless our work and help us put our best efforts into helping.

Wrap Up

Chat about what "work ethic" means in your family and how you can develop good work habits.

Responsibility

Family Beatitude: Happy is the family who accepts responsibilities, for they will be trustworthy.

Focus: Responsibility

Weekly Bible Verse: *"Those who have been given a trust must prove that they are faithful."* – 1 Corinthians 4:2

Activity Options on Responsibility

☐ If there's an area where a family member is not being responsible, make and post a checklist. This can be anything from the morning routine of making the bed to washing the kitchen floor. Add a star each time the individual follows the checklist. Younger children may need pictures for how to do each step.

☐ Fill chore buckets with needed supplies, such as window cleaner and paper towels for cleaning glass and mirrors.

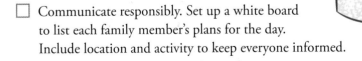

☐ Communicate responsibly. Set up a white board to list each family member's plans for the day. Include location and activity to keep everyone informed.

King of the Floor 1-2 minutes

"Wow! What a great job washing the floor. I didn't even have to remind you."

Joseph grinned. "I read the chore chart. I also let Thomas watch and explained how to wash the floor."

"Well, that makes you 'King of the Floor Washing.' "

Joseph worked hard to be king of each chore he had on his list. Soon, his nine-year-old sister followed his example to become Queen of Making Beds and other chores. As the eldest siblings, they helped teach the younger ones how to do their work. Mom added a few more responsibilities to the tasks and gave them a bonus when they did them. For cleaning floors, extra tasks included putting the chairs and other pieces of furniture back in place, wringing out the mop, and putting the mop and broom away.

The younger children clamored to be royal workers too. So Thomas took on the role of "Goodnight King" to make sure everyone brushed his or her teeth. He tucked each one into bed. All the children checked the chore chart and chose to do their tasks without being reminded. They wanted to keep their crowns for jobs well done.

Bible Story Connection 2 minutes

Read about Jonah in the book of Jonah 1:1-3,17; 3:1-5. He ran from the task God gave him to do. We need to be doing what God wants us to do. Get out your list of family chores. Does anyone need to get up and do one after devotion time?

Chat Prompts: Options

"Jonah ran away from the Lord. He headed for Tarshish."

– Jonah 1:3a

God gave Jonah a job to do, but Jonah refused. After lots of trouble, Jonah finally accepted the job and helped many people. Talk about times someone didn't follow through on a responsibility and discuss what happened.

MORE TIME?

"Will you thank the servant because he did what he was told to do? It's the same with you. Suppose you have done everything you were told to do. Then you should say, 'We are not worthy to serve you. We have only done our duty.' " – Luke 17:9-10

Do children expect their parents to work and provide a home for them? Chat about each person's responsibilities. Should a person expect a reward for being responsible?

"The foolish ones took their lamps but didn't take any olive oil with them." – Matthew 25:3

This scripture is from a parable about ten young women. They went to a wedding and needed to bring lamps. Five didn't take enough oil, and that caused them to miss the celebration. Without oil, their lamps went out. That's like letting a cell phone die or not having batteries for a flashlight. Chat about how being prepared is also part of being responsible. How should each person be prepared for school and home?

Scrapbook/Prayer Journal Options

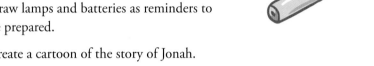

Add art as reminders of being responsible.

- Draw lamps and batteries as reminders to be prepared.

- Create a cartoon of the story of Jonah.

- Draw crowns for each family member. Write in chores that person does.

Prayer

Father, help us take our responsibilities seriously. Help us follow through when we give our word.

Wrap Up
Chat about how being responsible helps people.

Cooperation

Family Beatitude: Happy is the family who cooperates, for they will be team players.

Focus: Cooperation

Weekly Bible Verse: *"Two people are better than one. They can help each other in everything they do."* – Ecclesiastes 4:9

Activity Options on Teamwork

☐ Set up some team tasks, such as painting a fence or a room. Set up different ways family members can work together to accomplish the goal. For example, younger ones can provide snacks and bottles of water.

☐ Enjoy a cooperative food-making activity. Blindfold one person and have another guide that person to make an ice-cream sundae, sandwich, or other snack.

☐ Create an obstacle course. Have two family members do the course holding hands or with two of their legs tied together.

Hurricane Repairs 1-2 minutes

"Becky, clean up this mess!" Two-year-old Daniel imitated his mother when his teen sister took him to the top of the stairs.

Below them, broken glass lay in inches of water, furniture had toppled and slammed into other pieces, and pictures had fallen off the wall.

Mom called up, "Let's gather together. I don't know when Dad will be able to fly home. The airport is closed. We need to do what we can."

Becky said, "I don't think Daniel can do much except repeat you. I'm the oldest, so I can probably do the most."

One of her brothers protested. "Well, I'm the strongest, so I can probably do the most."

"This is not a competition," Mom said. "Look at all the damage the rushing winds of one big hurricane did in a few hours. I even have an idea of a way Daniel can help."

"I help!" little Daniel said.

Soon the older boys headed outside with Daniel's wagon to pick up debris. The girls put on boat shoes and started picking up broken glass inside the house. Mom put boat shoes on Daniel and once all the broken glass inside was picked up, she opened a window, gave him a pail,  and showed him how to scoop up water and dump it out the window.

At noon, Becky sliced bread she'd baked before the storm. They sat around snacking and talking about the damages and the work they'd done. They laughed about silly things like the one picture still hanging on the wall. Mom read from the book of Nehemiah about the people working together to repair the broken wall around Jerusalem.

Bible Story Connection 2 minutes

Read about the picture story Jesus told where he is the vine and his followers are the branches (John 15:5-8). Fill a plate with grapes and talk about how they grow on vines. Use a rope and have members hold on to it while you walk around the house. Note how the rope keeps you connected.

Chat Prompts: Options

● *"Two people are better than one. They can help each other in everything they do. Suppose either of them falls down. Then the one can help the other one up. But suppose a person falls down and doesn't have anyone to help them up. Then feel sorry for that person!"* – Ecclesiastes 4:10

Talk about the importance of a team and having helpful people in your life. How can your family members support one another? How can you cheer on teammates, especially your family members as they work or play?

MORE TIME?

● *"We rebuilt the wall. We repaired it until all of it was half as high as we wanted it to be. The people worked with all their heart."* – Nehemiah 4:6

Nehemiah shows the great results of cooperation. The wall around Jerusalem lay in ruins for seventy years. Then Nehemiah encouraged the Israelites to cooperate and work together. They rebuilt the wall in fifty-two days (Nehemiah 6:15). What does your family need to repair in relationships or projects? How can your family work together to do great things?

● *"Two people are better than one. They can help each other in everything they do."* – Ecclesiastes 4:9

Talk about how your family can encourage other people in your life to work together at school, work, or in the neighborhood.

Scrapbook/Prayer Journal Options

Picture cooperation with art.

- Draw a broken wall and a rebuilt wall, and write about cooperation.

- Draw and write about a family project.

- Add pictures of obstacles and ways cooperation helps you overcome them.

Prayer

Lord, help us develop a cooperative attitude and spirit. Help us reach out when someone needs our help.

Wrap Up

What did you learn about cooperation and teamwork this week?

Sprinkles of Joy

Family Beatitude: Happy is the family who sprinkles joy into lives, for they will laugh.

Focus: Passing joy to others

Weekly Bible Verse: *"Don't forget to do good. Don't forget to share with others. God is pleased with those kinds of offerings."* – Hebrews 13:16

Activity Options on Sprinkling Joy into Lives

☐ Leave out notecards with stickers and markers. Encourage everyone to write notes to make people smile. Post the notes.

☐ Serve one another in little ways. Suggestions for family members: make snacks, do someone else's chore, or let someone choose what game to play with you.

☐ Parents randomly give children a little blessing (a sticker, special dessert, little toy, staying up an extra fifteen minutes, a new book or story).

☐ Add joyful notes or jokes on someone's pillow or in his or her pocket or lunchbox.

Surprise 1-2 minutes

Michael received his first paycheck for a "real" job. He worked after school a few days a week at a garden shop. He walked to the bank to cash his check and stopped at a store before walking home.

After dinner, Michael said, "Stick around everyone. I have a surprise. Close your eyes until I tell you to open them."

Everyone listened to Michael striding around, opening doors, and making scraping noises with something metal. Finally, he said, "Open your eyes!"

Everyone yelled, "Ice cream! Wow! Thanks, Michael."

Michael grinned. "I wanted to celebrate my first paycheck and surprise everyone."

They all clapped and congratulated Michael. His dad asked him to share about his job and what he liked about it. Michael mentioned that he liked the hard work of lifting bags of fertilizer because it would strengthen his muscles.

Michael used part of his first paycheck to treat his family to ice cream cones. He'd picked a few favorite flavors, including mint chocolate chip and cookie dough, and served everyone. His family had a tradition of sharing a blessing with everyone when something good happened. When Dad got a raise or someone received a special blessing, they all celebrated. They also found ways to bless one another often in little ways.

Bible Story Connection 2 minutes

Read Nehemiah 8:10-17. The Israelite people are rejoicing and saying that God's strength is their joy. They were camping out and remembering how God brought them out of slavery. What has happened in your family lately to rejoice about? Spend time remembering and celebrating together.

Chat Prompts: Options

● *"I have told you this so that you will have the same joy that I have. I also want your joy to be complete."* – John 15:11

Jesus spoke to his disciples about following him. He wanted them to be filled with joy—the joy that comes from God. Talk about how growing close to God as a family increases joy. What do you do as a family to grow close to God?

MORE TIME?

● *"May the Lord our God always be pleased with us. Lord, make what we do succeed. Please make what we do succeed."*
– Psalm 90:17

These words remind us to please God, and God can give us success. What are you doing as a family that is pleasing God? Pray this verse as a family.

● *"A cheerful heart makes you healthy. but a broken spirit dries you up."* – Proverbs 17:22

God wants us to have joy and be cheerful. Chat about what helps you smile and feel joy. How does your family cheer up a member who is sad or feeling ill?

Scrapbook/Prayer Journal Options

Add art to show joy and reflect what your family does to sprinkle joy in people's lives.

- Add a sun with a happy face. Write jokes or reasons your family laughs.

- Paint with bright watercolors. Add a note that God loves you and that your family members love each other.

- Draw a share icon and ideas of how your family passes joy around.

Prayer

Father, we thank you for our family. Help each of us sprinkle joy in the lives of everyone around us.

Wrap Up
Talk about what surprises you enjoyed this week.

Knowledge

Family Beatitude: Happy is the family who pursues knowledge, for they will enjoy learning.

Focus: Eagerness to learn

Weekly Bible Verse: *"Your heart will become wise. Your mind will delight in knowledge."* – Proverbs 2:10

Activity Options on Eagerness to Learn

☐ Make frequent trips to the library and bookstores. Let children earn books from chores and activities. Snap photos of trips and holding books they enjoy.

☐ Provide a taste of fun and learning on various topics through experiments, interesting facts, and field trips. Match books to favorite topics.

☐ Hold a show-and-tell evening to let children share about their interests. Let them show and talk about a book they've read related to their interests.

☐ Check online together to find sites related to topics of interest or ones your children are studying in school. Let your children present something new they learned at dinner.

The Library 1-2 minutes

"Mom, may we go to the library? I finished the books I checked out last week." Nine-year-old Kalani held up a pile of books.

"Sure. Let me get the books I finished."

Once at the library, Kalani searched the children's shelves and returned to his mom. "I can't find more books on electricity. I've read them all. I don't know what other books to get today."

"You're a good reader. Let's look online and see what else they have. There are also books on that topic in the adult sections."

"Will they let me check-out books written for adults?"

"Sure. All the books are here for anyone who wants to read them." Kalani watched his mom log on and type in "electricity." Up popped a long list of books. He wrote down the numbers of some titles that looked interesting. His mom helped him find the books on the shelves by their catalog numbers. He opened each one to make sure he could understand what the author wrote. He chose a few books and smiled. "There are a lot more books for adults than there are for kids. I think I'll be in this section a lot more!"

When he handed the books to the librarian to check them out, she grinned. "You must be a good reader. You get a load of books almost every week."

"I like learning—especially about science."

"Well, keep coming back. We buy books according to what people check out. I know you've checked out just about every science book in the children's section, so we'll be getting new science books soon."

James smiled. "That's good news."

Bible Story Connection 2 minutes

Read 2 Chronicles 1:1-10, which talks about the wisest man who ever lived. He first worshipped God. When God asked what he wanted, Solomon didn't ask for money or things for himself. He simply wanted wisdom to lead God's people well. Put a dictionary or laptop on the table. Talk about the knowledge it contains. Open it up and learn something new together.

Chat Prompts: Options

- *"A heart that understands what is right looks for knowledge. But the mouths of foolish people feed on what is foolish."* – Proverbs 15:14

Talk about what a person gains by studying and learning. Talk about what subjects are easier for each person and what ones are harder. Discuss why Bible study is an important part of learning.

MORE TIME?

- *"You have felt secure in your evil ways. You have said, 'No one sees what I'm doing.' Your wisdom and knowledge lead you astray. You say to yourself, 'I am like a god. No one is greater than I am.'"* – Isaiah 47:10

God's people turned away from God as they gained worldly knowledge. They didn't think they needed him. Today many people believe science has all the answers so they don't need God. How can technology and science sometimes influence people away from believing in God? What do you think about the idea that science is revealing God's great planning and creativity?

- *"Don't just listen to the word. You fool yourselves if you do that. You must do what it says."* – James 1:22

The book of James encourages people to ask God if they need wisdom. Why is it important to have more than head knowledge? How does it take faith to believe in things you can't see? How can you apply what you learn to life? How do you live the words in the Bible and become doers of the Word?

Scrapbook/Prayer Journal Options

Add books and other art to picture the love of knowledge.

- Draw books and write your favorite titles on them.

- Draw pictures related to each person's favorite subject.

- Add pictures about school and words about learning.

Prayer

Father, help us view books as adventures in learning. Help us apply our knowledge wisely and be enthusiastic about growing in wisdom and in you.

Wrap Up

Talk about the importance of knowledge and the adventure of learning.

Comfort

Family Beatitude: Happy is the family who has good neighbors, for they will be comforted in times of need.

Focus: Comfort

Weekly Bible Verse: *"[God] comforts us in all our troubles. Now we can comfort others when they are in trouble. We ourselves receive comfort from God."* – 2 Corinthians 1:4

Activity Options on Giving Comfort

☐ Enjoy group hugs often, especially when someone is feeling sad or upset. Give out little pompons to remind everyone to cheer for each other and give them hugs.

☐ For young ones, use guided play with dolls and stuffed animals to help develop compassion. Say, "Oh, this baby is crying" or "The bear fell and got hurt." Ask your children to give comfort. Encourage them to use words and actions.

☐ Make cards that express comfort. Hold a time to make cards to console others who may be sick, experienced loss, or have other needs. Mail or pass them to friends in need.

Little Nurse 1-2 minutes

Frank came in crying. "I fell down. I'm bleeding!"

"Mom, I'll take care of Frankie!" eight-year-old Marie yelled. She dropped her doll on a chair and ran to her brother. "Let me see. Ooh! That must hurt, but I can make you better. I'll get a bandage and some other things. Just sit quietly right here. Put your leg on the stool to raise it up. That helps stop the bleeding."

Marie ran into the bathroom. She grabbed the first-aid kit and wet a washcloth. She came back into the kitchen.

"Okay, Frankie. First, I'm going to clean the cut and see how it looks. I remember how much I hurt when I fell and cut my knee on a rock."

Frank yelled ouch a little, and a few more tears slid down his cheeks as Marie gently dabbed his wound.

"Now I need to put on some medicine so it won't get infected. It will sting just a few seconds. It will stop by the time I end a song." She sang "Jesus Loves You." Frank sobbed along with her.

"Look, Frank. I have a special bandage for you. It's got turtles on it."
Frank sniffed a little bit.

"Oh, I forgot one thing." Marie kissed the bandage on his knee. "Mommy can kiss your cut too. That will make it feel even better."

Frank said, "Thanks. I do feel better."

"I can get some ice to put on your knee. Would you like the bunny-boo-boo?"

Frank nodded.

Marie placed their special ice pack on her brother's knee.

Mom walked in and said, "Great job, Marie. You'll make a good doctor or nurse when you grow up."

"I've been practicing on my dolls, but a real person is even better."

Bible Story Connection 2 minutes

Read 2 Corinthians 7:6-7 and Philippians 4:14-17. The apostle Paul talks about the comfort of friends. Titus visited him and brought news of friends. People had sent Paul gifts when he was in prison. Pass out your sympathy or friendship cards. Write notes to people who need comfort.

Chat Prompts: Options

● *"We gave you hope and strength. We comforted you. We really wanted you to live in a way that is worthy of God."* – 1 Thessalonians 2:12a

Paul is talking to the people in Thessalonica that he had taught about God. He talks about working with them and comforting them. Who are the people in your life (Church, school, neighborhood, or family) that teaches, comforts and encourages you to do things God's way. Make a list and tell them thank you.

MORE TIME?

● *"[Jesus said,] 'I have prayed for you, Simon. I have prayed that your faith will not fail. When you have turned back, help your brothers to be strong."* – Luke 22:32

Jesus told Peter that he would deny him, and then Jesus went on to say that when Peter returned to his faith, he could use his experience to help other believers. Jesus knew before it happened that Peter would fail but recover, and the process would make him a better person. How do your failures, hardships, and problems help you comfort others?

● *"[The LORD says,] 'As a mother comforts her child, I will comfort you. You will find comfort in Jerusalem."*
– Isaiah 66:13

God promises to comfort you. Remember to ask him to help dry your tears and heal your heart when you are hurting. Share a time you felt comforted by God.

Scrapbook/Prayer Journal Options

Illustrate what comfort means to you in this book.

- Draw bandages and write words that express comfort.

- Draw a stuffed bear. Write words of comfort around it, such as "snuggles" and "cuddles."

- Draw arms for hugs.

Prayer

Lord, you are the God of comfort. Heal our hearts when we hurt. Bring us friends and family to comfort us when we need it.

Wrap Up

Chat about what you learned about comfort and the different ways to help people feel better.

Fall Fun

> **Family Beatitude:** Happy is the family who celebrates harvest season, for they will appreciate healthy food.
>
> **Focus:** Harvest fun
>
> **Weekly Bible Verse:** *"Brothers and sisters, be patient until the Lord comes. See how the farmer waits for the land to produce its rich crop. See how patient the farmer is for the fall and spring rains."* – James 5:7

Activity Options for Harvest Season

☐ Pick local produce or shop at a farmer's market for produce. Enjoy the fresh pickings. Discuss how to tell if different fruits and vegetables are ripe.

☐ Apples grow in every state. Cut one crosswise to see how the seeds form a star. Talk about all the ways you can use apples for eating and games. Try a new apple recipe.

☐ Collect colored leaves, acorns, and other natural items and make centerpieces to celebrate the harvest season.

☐ Make popcorn and have a family gathering to talk about what is grown locally. Make plans to grow something in the next growing season where you live. Discuss what is needed for plants to grow.

Apple Picking 1-2 minutes

Jerry ran into the house holding a red apple. "Look! The apples are getting ripe. I thought they would never finish growing and turn red." He washed the fruit. *Crunch!* He took a big bite. "Yeah! We can start picking them. Where's a basket?"

Jerry and his sister gathered a bushel of apples. Their cousins came by and helped. Over the next week, they picked more bushels of the bright-red apples. *Buzz!* They had to put on bug spray when yellow jackets decided they also wanted some of the sweet fruit.

Grandpa took some apples to the cider mill and had them pressed into delicious cider to drink. Jerry's mom baked pies and froze some to enjoy during the coming winter.

The children had watched the apple trees since spring. First a few buds popped out, and then sweet-smelling, pink, apple blossoms opened up. Bumblebees buzzed around to pollinate the flowers. Robins made a nest

in one tree and hatched babies there. Then little green balls began to grow on the tree. It took from spring until autumn for the apples to be ready to eat.

The entire family enjoyed harvest time. They filled a basket with apples to decorate the table and enjoyed games such as dunking for apples and apple-rolling races.

Bible Story Connection 2 minutes

Put bread crumbs on the table. Read about wise creatures, including ants, that harvest food (Proverbs 30:24-31). Chat about how ants carry off even the tiniest crumb to save it. What are ways you can save things and not waste food or other items? Talk about the wisdom and wonder of the creatures mentioned in the passage.

Chat Prompts: Options

● *"Begin with the 15th day of the seventh month. That is after you have gathered your crops. On that day celebrate the LORD's Feast of Booths for seven days. The first day is a day of rest. The eighth day is also a day of rest."* – Leviticus 23:39

God wanted his people to celebrate the harvest. This gave them time to thank him for the produce and his creation. How can your family show thankfulness for all that God is providing?

MORE TIME?

● *"As long as the earth lasts, there will always be a time to plant and a time to gather the crops. As long as the earth lasts, there will always be cold and heat. There will always be summer and winter, day and night."* – Genesis 8:22

After the flood, God promised not to destroy the earth with a flood again. He mentioned that seasons would continue. Chat about what you like about each season. What is each person's favorite season and why?

● *"There is a time for everything. There's a time for everything that is done on earth."* – Ecclesiastes 3:1

Talk about the seasons of a person's life. People often try to do too much at once; instead, they should choose wisely. What can you do now, and what should you wait to do in another season of life to reach your full potential and do the best job possible?

Scrapbook/Prayer Journal Options

Illustrate the joy of the harvest in your book.

- Draw leaves and color them. Add notes about how God colors your life with joy.

- Use apples to add apple prints to the pages. Write about each person's star qualities.

- Draw each person's favorite vegetable or fruit.

Prayer

Lord, thanks for all the produce you created and the seasons you established. Help us enjoy your creation.

Wrap Up

Chat about the fun of the changing seasons.

Worldviews

Family Beatitude: Happy is the family who holds a biblical worldview, for they will be in God's will.

Focus: Biblical view versus worldviews

Weekly Bible Verse: *"The wisdom of this world is foolish in God's eyes. It is written, 'God catches wise people in their own evil plans.'"*
— 1 Corinthians 3:19

Activity Options on Biblical Views

☐ After an outing, ask each person to write about the experience. Share what each person writes and how each one saw different things or may have understood things differently. These reveal part of developing different perspectives.

☐ Read news articles and watch the news. Compare the points of view to God's perspective based on what you read in the Bible.

☐ Toss a ball up and watch it fall back to earth. Talk about gravity. Make a list of other known truths, such as one plus one equals two. Discuss how these "scientific laws" are part of how God created the universe.

☐ Watch a modern TV show together and look for anything that goes against God's teaching. Help them learn to be careful with what they watch.

FAMILY DEVOTION
• READ ALOUD •

Real Wisdom 1 minute

Rebecca begged, "My birthday is coming. Please buy the doll piano for me that I saw on TV. It's so cool."

Her daddy replied, "They do make it look great. I don't think you'd play with it long and it might break fast.

"But I will love it. I'll use it every day. I could even learn to play music."

Her mom said, "Lots of times they have to advertise things to get them to sell. It doesn't mean they are the best items. You stopped piano lessons because you didn't want to practice."

"But this one is tiny and cute."

Her parents gave her the toy piano and several other gifts they thought she'd enjoy more. She played with the piano a few times and then it collected dust. She used her jump rope, art supplies, and other items all the time.

Rebecca's dad said, "I notice you're not using that toy piano much, but I'm happy you enjoy your other presents."

"You were right. It wasn't the best gift. You knew what I would really like. How did you get to be so smart?"

"Wisdom can take time to develop. I read the Bible and pray for wisdom. The wisdom from God is not like what people say is great or wise in this world. That's why commercials can be misleading. God's word is always true. I also listened and learned from my parents. And I learned from my mistakes."

"Did Mom do that too?"

"Yes."

"I learned not to want something because it's on TV. I better keep reading my Bible. I want to be wise like you and mom. I want to have God's wisdom."

Dad gave Rebecca a hug and said, "That's great. I'd like to make something with you. Where are those art supplies?"

Bible Story Connection 2 minutes

Read in Exodus 5:1-2 how the Egyptian Pharaoh thought he was greater than God and didn't need to listen to him. Exodus 6:1 shows God's response. Finally, the Pharaoh let God's people go. You can read that in Exodus 12:31. But it didn't happen until God sent many plagues on the Egyptians. Pharaoh thought he ruled the world, and he only looked at his own worldview. His view left out God and his power. What things do people think are more important than God these days? Make a list as a family.

Chat Prompts: Options

● *"The wisdom of this world is foolish in God's eyes. It is written, 'God catches wise people in their own evil plans.'"* – 1 Corinthians 3:19

The Bible verse for this week tells us people tend to think they are wise when they are not. If we are not following God we are following ourself. God calls that foolish. How do you know what you are doing and thinking is God's way? Write down ways to find out what is God's way of thinking.

MORE TIME?

● *"Do not love the world or anything in it. If anyone loves the world, love for the Father is not in them."* – 1 John 2:15

How you live reveals your heart. How do you spend your time and money? Discuss examples of that as seen on TV, on the news, in movies, and through games.

● *"Don't let any evil talk come out of your mouths. Say only what will help to build others up and meet their needs. Then what you say will help those who listen."* – Ephesians 4:29

Others may hold a different view of what is right or wrong. Create a checklist of how to decide if what someone is saying is true or not. If they don't see things God's way, how can you help them see the truth in a loving way?

Scrapbook/Prayer Journal Options

Draw symbols that remind you to follow God and not the world.

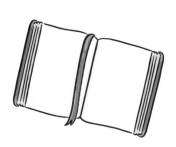

- Draw a Bible and write what truth means to God.

- Draw the path of a ball tossed in the air and write how it relates to truth.

- Draw a mouth and words that are good, such as compliments and truth.

Prayer

Father, help us apply your Word to our daily lives. Show us how to follow your worldview all the time.

Wrap Up

Discuss ways to remain faithful to God and his Word.

Understanding Messages

Family Beatitude: Happy is the family who develops discernment, for they will choose good over evil.

Focus: Correctly processing media and other influences

Weekly Bible Verse: *"Say no to every kind of evil."*
– 1 Thessalonians 5:22

Activity Options on Understanding Messages

☐ Analyze different magazines and the ads in them. Describe the people in them (age, nationality, sex, looks). What are they trying to sell? What attitudes are they revealing? How are they trying to get you to want the product? What is the truth? How should you decide what to buy?

☐ Analyze television shows together as a family. What is said and what people do. List any compliments, teasing, bullying, and praises said. List actions that helped people and ones that hurt, actions that follow God's rules, and ones that break them. Write down if there was kissing or other shows of affection.

☐ Go online together to check out Christian-based reviews of movies, books, music, and games (movieguide.org; pluggedin.com). Use them to find good family movies and wholesome games.

What's Really Happening?

1-2 minutes

"I picked up the latest book of the series you like."

"Hooray! When can I read it?" Sally grinned.

"I'll read it tonight and give it to you tomorrow after you finish your schoolwork and chores."

Sally and her mom had an agreement. Her mom read her books and watched the shows she watched. Then they chatted about them. They discussed how the characters behaved and the words they used.

Sally said, "I read the last book and guessed ahead who did it. I got it right!"

Her mom said, "Yes. And did you notice who acted kind and who teased or made bad comments?"

"Yes. That one boy was really nasty. What a loser."

"It's time for your favorite show." They turned on the television and sat down.

When they heard some swear words, Sally said, "Mom, you always seem to tune in the only time anyone swears. The show really isn't that bad. It's just a few words."

"Why don't I make some brownies for us?"

"Great."

"I will add just a little bit of dog poop. Not much…just a teeny bit."

"Yuck. I wouldn't eat that. Oh, I get it. I'll turn off the show. Just a little bit does ruin things."

Bible Story Connection 2 minutes

Read about how even the wisest man made mistakes (1 Kings 11:4-13). Solomon had lots of knowledge, but he didn't always follow God. He let people influence his heart away from God and allowed idols to come into his life. With your family, put money, chocolate, fortune cookies, and jewelry on the table. Talk about how we sometimes let things get in the way of putting God first. We let them become idols.

Chat Prompts: Options

"Your eye is like a lamp for your body. Suppose your eyes are healthy. Then your whole body also is full of light. But suppose your eyes can't see well. Then your body also is full of darkness." – Luke 11:34

What we see goes into our mind and heart and changes us. How does media impact your mind? How can you control what influences you?

MORE TIME?

"Make sure no one controls you. They will try to control you by using false reasoning that has no meaning. Their ideas depend on human teachings. They also depend on the basic spiritual powers of this world. They don't depend on Christ."
– Colossians 2:8

How do the authors of games, television programs, and books attempt to influence or control your mind? What can you do to be sure God is in control?

"Suppose people lead one of these little ones to sin. It would be better for those people to be thrown into the sea with a millstone tied around their neck." – Luke 17:2
Jesus spoke these words. He was talking about creating stumbling blocks or things that try to lead people away from God. Why must you consider other people, especially children, when choosing what to watch, read, and play with?

Scrapbook/Prayer Journal Options

Add illustrations to the pages to reflect your thoughts on outside influences.

- Draw books, TVs, DVDs, and musical notes. Write pledges to keep away from ungodly input.

- Draw eyes and ears and write notes about what is good input.

- Draw a traffic light and write a note to stop and pay attention to a TV show or book before choosing to give it a green light.

Prayer

Father, keep our minds healthy and pure. Help us make good choices on what to see and hear.

Wrap Up

Talk about ways to guard your hearts, ears, eyes, and minds.

Service

Family Beatitude: Happy is the family who serves others, for people will see Christ in their actions.

Focus: Serving people

Weekly Bible Verse: *"Be like the Son of Man. He did not come to be served. Instead, he came to serve others. He came to give his life as the price for setting many people free."* – Matthew 20:28

Activity Options on Serving People

☐ Service begins at home. List ways family members can serve one another. Examples: reading to siblings, doing chores for each other, helping cook, and making someone else's bed.

☐ Check out community needs where you can serve as a family. These may include collecting food for food pantries, cleaning up parks, and contributing to toy collections for missions.

☐ If there's a disaster in your state, find out ways to help. It may mean collecting and sending canned goods with can openers, giving toys to children, or providing school supplies.

☐ Check your family's service attitudes. Practice smiling and greeting people, offering encouragement, and being humble enough to do anything needed.

Pitching In 1-2 minutes

Four days after a major hurricane hit the area, a big shout rang out on Tessa's street when the lights came on. The families stood outside where they'd been barbecuing food thawed in freezers that no longer had power. Their phones worked now too.

They checked with neighborhood friends, and discovered one family with health problems who still had no electricity. Sherry's family had to fill their generator every four hours, and continually needed more gas. Tessa said she could stay at a friend's home so that family could stay in her room. So, Sherry and her girls drove over. Sherry switched into her wheelchair and rolled into Tessa's house. Sherry's husband remained behind to work on repairs.

They discovered that many other friends had no power and were washing clothes by hand and hanging them up to dry. People dropped

off smelly clothes, including some that had sat for days after the storm. Tessa's family labeled each bundle and started sorting, washing, and folding clothes. Their family room filled with baskets of fresh-smelling clothes. As families dropped off clothes, they also took showers and enjoyed homemade cookies and iced tea. Sherry and her girls helped fold clothes.

Tessa came down one morning in a one-piece bathing suit after a few weeks of washing clothes. She said, "This is my work outfit. I'll stay in my bathing suit all day. There's no school yet, and this makes fewer clothes to wash, sort, and fold." Her family decided to suit up too and cheerfully continued helping friends.

Bible Story Connection 2-3 minutes

Jesus served his friends. Read how he washed his disciple's feet (John 13:1-15). Place a basin of water, towels, and foot lotion on the table. Wash each other's feet.

Chat Prompts: Options

● *"Serve your masters with all your heart. Work as serving the Lord and not as serving people."* – Ephesians 6:7

How can thinking of serving God help you better serve a grumpy or unhappy person? What are little ways you can serve people?

● *"We are God's creation. He created us to belong to Christ Jesus. Now we can do good works. Long ago God prepared these works for us to do."* – Ephesians 2:10

God created everyone, and he wants us all to help and love one another. Talk about ways Jesus served people. Discuss how God's plans for us include opportunities to serve each other. What can you do to help people this week?

● *"We remember you when we pray to our God and Father. Your work is produced by your faith. Your service is the result of your love. Your strength to continue comes from your hope in our Lord Jesus Christ."* – 1 Thessalonians 1:3

How does faith help you want to help others? How does loving other people make it easier to serve them? How can serving people who have little or nothing bring them hope?

● *"Be wise in the way you act toward outsiders. Make the most of every opportunity."* – Colossians 4:5

How do you choose to spend your time? How is free time also an opportunity to serve? What does your calendar look like? Is there room left to help people? If not, what changes can you make?

Scrapbook/Prayer Journal Options

Add artwork as reminders to serve others.

- Draw smiles for good attitudes.

- Add pennies as reminders that there are always people who need help and have less than you do. Write notes of what you can give.

- Draw pictures related to service your family does or will do for other people.

Prayer

Lord, help us reach out to serve people, especially those in need. Help us be cheerful givers of our time and energy.

Wrap Up

Talk about any continued service you do as a family. What helps you stay committed and cheerful?

Friendships

Family Beatitude: Happy is the family who cultivates friendships, for they will have rich lives.

Focus: Friendships

Weekly Bible Verse: *"David finished talking with Saul. After that, Jonathan and David became close friends. Jonathan loved David just as he loved himself."* – 1 Samuel 18:1

Activity Options on Friendship

☐ Practice greeting people. Think of questions to ask when you meet someone. Getting to know people is the start of building friendships. Be ready to exchange contact information and discuss available times to get together.

☐ Practice listening skills and good ways to respond to questions. Look at the person and really listen. Make a chart of emotions to notice in a friend and possible responses.

☐ Take photos with friends and make friendship booklets together. Write or draw about good times and bad times. Note how your friends helped you plan favorite activities together.

☐ Plan a friendship outing. Discuss with your parents what would be fun to do together, such as meeting in a park, going to a movie, or having lunch together. Carry out the plans.

Longtime Friends 1-2 minutes

"May Jimmy come over and play?" Daniel asked his mom.

"Sure. Do you remember when you first became good friends?"

"I remember playing with him in a big wagon."

"Yes. His mom and I both taught at Vacation Bible School. The two of you kept trying to escape the nursery and run off together. We finally put both of you in a wagon and kept you near us. You liked being pulled around. You chattered together. His mom taught cooking and gave you snacks. I taught art and gave you things to make."

"Then Jimmy's mom died when we were five. That was so sad."

"Yes, it was sad. She was my friend. But we helped Jimmy and his brother and their dad."

"We picked Jimmy up from his school once a week and got his little brother from the babysitter. Jimmy and I did our homework and then played all afternoon. We'll always be friends even though sometimes he can be crazy. We have fun together."

The two boys enjoyed scouts and church activities as they grew up. They flipped over in canoes, stood up against bullies, and helped each other with scout projects. Daniel helped Jimmy when his car broke down, and Jimmy gave Daniel furniture when he rented a place to live.

There's a close friendship mentioned in the Bible too. Jonathan and David became instant friends when they met. They shared what they owned. When Jonathan's dad, King Saul, wanted to kill David, Jonathan protected his friend. They hugged each other when they had to part. David remained loyal to Jonathan's family after his friend was killed.

Bible Story Connection 2-3 minutes

Read about people who really helped their friend in Mark 2:1-12. They wanted to bring him to Jesus to be healed. What did they do when they couldn't get close enough? What happened to the sick man? Put a saw and a piece of wood on the table and talk about how the men climbed on top of the house and made a hole in the roof. Go outside and take turns sawing the wood.

Chat Prompts: Options

- *"They could not get him close to Jesus because of the crowd. So they made a hole by digging through the roof above Jesus. Then they lowered the man through it on a mat."* – Mark 2:4

Wow! These friends really wanted to help their physically challenged friend. Read more of the story to see what Jesus did. What do you do when a friend needs help? Does your friend know Jesus? How can you help your friend get to know Jesus better?

MORE TIME?

- *"I do not call you slaves anymore. Slaves do not know their master's business. Instead, I have called you friends. I have told you everything I learned from my Father."* – John 15:15

Jesus wants to be your friend. Have you accepted his friendship? How do you get closer to your friends? What can you do to build your friendship with him?

- *"Godly people are careful about the friends they choose. But the way of sinners leads them down the wrong path."*

– Proverbs 12:26

Friends can lead us the wrong way. When has a friend gotten you in trouble? When has a friend hurt you? How should you respond? When do you decide you need to make a new friend and stay away from a bad friend? Check out a few other verses about friends: Proverbs 22:24; 27:9. Discuss how to make wise choices in choosing friends.

Scrapbook/Prayer Journal Options

Add artwork to celebrate friendships.

- Draw hearts and write the names of friends of each family member in the hearts.

- Draw a footprint and write about choosing friends who are good and follow Jesus.

- Draw praying hands. Write about praying for friends.

Prayer

Lord, help us make good friends and keep them. Help us be ready to be kind and forgiving to friends and to listen to them well.

Wrap Up

Name the best things about your friends. Chat about ways to make new friends and keep the old ones.

Priorities

> **Family Beatitude:** Happy is the family who sets priorities, for they will have time to be together.
>
> **Focus:** Setting priorities
>
> **Weekly Bible Verse:** *"But put God's kingdom first. Do what he wants you to do. Then all those things will also be given to you."*
> — *Matthew 6:33*

Activity Options on Setting Priorities

☐ Take a glass jar and fill it with rocks. Add pebbles. Add soil. And then add water. Use it to talk about priorities. Note that the big things had to go in first. That represents what's most important. The little things can fit in during spare minutes. What are the most important things that need to be a priority?

☐ Look at your calendar. How much time is already scheduled? How much free time is available? Every time you write in a future activity, you are charging against your available time. Avoid getting into time debt.

☐ List what's most important to you. Note what must be done, such as cooking, cleaning, schoolwork, and jobs. Consider where you can save time, such as limiting playing games or television watching.

☐ Let each person list his or her goals and activities. Rank them by order of importance and then by favorites. See if there's time for all the goals and desires. Make sure to build in time for family fun.

I'm Not Done 1-2 minutes

"Son, is your report done? I see on the calendar it's due tomorrow."

"Not yet. I didn't have time."

"You're in trouble. You took time to play games and hang out with friends this afternoon. We're having a family ice-cream sundae evening and games, but you'll have to miss out and work on that report."

"I didn't know you had that planned. I would have done the homework sooner. Mom probably bought cookie dough ice cream and hot fudge syrup too."

"Ice cream fun is on the calendar. You need to pay attention, check the family calendar, and plan your time better. It's good to be prepared. It's also important to do a good job."

In the Old Testament, there's a problem in God's special city, Jerusalem, for His people the Israelites. Enemies burned the walls, destroyed the city, and captured the Israelites. Eventually a remnant of the Israelites returned to make repairs. They rebuilt the temple, but they procrastinated on the rest. For

seventy years, Jerusalem's walls remained piles of rubble. Nehemiah gave the Israelites a big pep talk. He pointed out the problem and encouraged them to get to work. He wanted them to focus on fixing the problem.

They responded, "Let's get to work!"

It's important to do more than put something on a calendar, to do more than just think about working on a task. You need to make it a priority, to get going and accomplish the job.

Bible Story Connection **2 minutes**

Have one parent read Luke 10:38-42 aloud while the other deliberately does distracting activities such as working or cleaning. Talk about the importance of putting God first. Now have the busy parent sit down and pay attention. Read the passage again. When was it easier to listen? Talk about Mary and Martha and their situation.

Chat Prompts: Options

● *"Put God's kingdom first. Do what he wants you to do. Then all those things will also be given to you."* – Matthew 6:31,33

God wants us to focus on doing his will first. He promises in this verse to take care of our needs. Talk about what things cause us to stop seeking God. How do we get distracted from God being our priority?

MORE TIME?

● *"Your heart will be where your riches are."* – Luke 12:34

Where you put your money, time, and talent reveals your heart and your priorities. Share how you spend your time. Do you need or want to consider making changes in how you manage your time?

● *"We pray he will give you the wisdom and understanding that the Spirit gives. Then you will be able to lead a life that is worthy of the Lord. We pray that you will please him in every way. So we want you to bear fruit in every good thing you do. We pray that you will grow to know God better."*
– Colossians 1:9-10

God wants you to bear fruit. In what ways are you fruitful? Do you have time for bearing fruit? What are you doing that pleases God?

Scrapbook/Prayer Journal Options

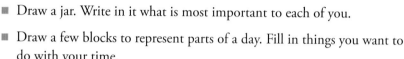

Let your artwork reflect your priorities.

- Draw a clock or watch. Add notes about how you spend your time.

- Draw a jar. Write in it what is most important to each of you.

- Draw a few blocks to represent parts of a day. Fill in things you want to do with your time.

Prayer

Father, thank you for giving us each a lifetime, whether it is long or short. Help us use our days wisely. We want to spend time with you, with our family, and with our friends.

Wrap Up
Discuss what memories you want to build in the time you have together this month.

Convictions

Family Beatitude: Happy is the family who learns discernment, for they will be guided by the Scriptures.

Focus: Godly discernment and convictions

Weekly Bible Verse: *"Make sure that in your hearts you honor Christ as Lord. Always be ready to give an answer to anyone who asks you about the hope you have. Be ready to give the reason for it. But do it gently and with respect."* – 1 Peter 3:15

Activity Options on Convictions and Tolerance

☐ Look at a favorite game system and talk about the possibility of throwing all the parts into the air and having them land in the right place to work together correctly. It took science and a designer to make the system. How much harder is it to make a living person, animal, or plant?

☐ Take turns sharing your reasons why you believe in God.

☐ Look up the Apostle's Creed and talk about each truth mentioned. These are basic Christian beliefs that are important to know and understand.

☐ Look online for archaeological proof of biblical history and truths. For example, look for documents about the "House of David," evidence of the Assyrian king Sargon (Isaiah 20:1), and records that indicate people at one time spoke the same language.

Questions that Inspire Thinking 1-2 minutes

"Dad, my friend said I'm intolerant because I believe in Jesus and because I value life and don't agree with abortion."

"Well, Son, some people call conviction and our freedom to believe in the Bible judgmental and intolerant. That doesn't change the truth in the Bible."

"What can I say when they push me to change my beliefs?"

"Do what Jesus did. Ask questions that make them think. Ask ones that show there are different beliefs, and they can't all be right."

"Like what?"

"Where do you think you came from?"

"Wow, those would be tough to answer for people who don't know Jesus."

"Yes. Hopefully these questions will get people thinking about their purpose here on Earth. They might consider the differences between good and evil, as well as their free will to choose between the two."

"Are those questions Jesus asked?"

"In the book of Job, God asked many questions about how the universe works. God wanted Job to know that God is all-knowing. Jesus used questions to get people thinking. He asked, 'What do you think about the Messiah? Whose son is he?' and 'Do you believe that I can do this?' You can look these questions up in Matthew 22:42 and 9:28."

Bible Story Connection 2 minutes

Read the book of Joshua 24:1-15. Joshua asks the people to again promise to follow God. He tells them that following God is a choice, and that he has made his choice. Take out a piece of paper and a pen. Draw a cross. Ask family members to sign their names if they agree to follow Jesus. If everyone signs it, post it where the family can see it often.

Chat Prompts: Options

● *"Do not judge other people. Then you will not be judged."* – Matthew 7:1 *"Here is the judgment. Light has come into the world, but people loved darkness instead of light. They loved darkness because what they did was evil."* – John 3:19-21

What is the difference between judging people and having strong beliefs in what is right? How can you believe the truth of Christ and still be patient with others who don't?

MORE TIME?

● *"Suppose someone teaches something different than I have taught. Suppose that person doesn't agree with the true teaching of our Lord Jesus Christ. Suppose they don't agree with godly teaching. Then that person is proud and doesn't understand anything. They like to argue more than they should. They can't agree about what words mean."* – 1 Timothy 6:3-4

How can you be at peace with people who disagree with your faith? What does it mean that someone "can't agree about what words mean"?

● *"Love must be honest and true. Hate what is evil. Hold on to what is good."* – Romans 12:9

How can you hold on to your faith when people argue and try to persuade you to follow the world's view or idols? Share ideas on responding to comments that Christianity or Christians are intolerant.

Scrapbook/Prayer Journal Options

Add artwork to show you believe in God with conviction. Also show that you are willing to politely listen to other people.

- Draw a Bible and art to represent the basic truths you believe.

- Draw an ear and words to show that people are free to express their beliefs.

- Draw a heart as a reminder to love all people, even those who disagree with your faith. That's called tolerance.

Prayer

Dear Lord, thank you for our faith in you. Help us to share our faith with love and to listen and communicate with those who disagree so they will want to know you too.

Wrap Up

Discuss what you think about truth and following Jesus. Remember, Jesus said, "I am the way and the truth and the life. No one comes to the Father except through me" (John 14:6).

Generosity

Family Beatitude: Happy is the family who is giving, for their hearts will be full of gratitude.

Focus: Generosity

Weekly Bible Verse: *"The godly are always giving and lending freely. Their children will be a blessing."* – Psalm 37:26

Activity Options on Generosity

☐ Buy or cut out a wooden heart. Color it with chalk paint and hang it up. Write in the name of a family member who gave something from the heart. Hopefully, names and deeds will continually change.

☐ Decide on an amount of money the family budget can use to donate to special causes. Gather the family together. Pray and then chat about where to give the money and how to divide it between the different causes.

☐ Set a giving example. Randomly call your children and give them a special treat, stickers, or coins. Let them know you simply want to bless them with a little gift, along with a hug, a smile, or an encouraging word.

☐ Involve children in projects to help others. Hold a yard sale or bake sale to raise money for charity, collect canned goods for a food pantry, or let children clean their closets to donate their gently used items to a mission.

Hannah's Heart 1-2 minutes

Hannah poured in the chocolate chips and stirred. Later, she helped take the warm cookies off the tray and pack them into a container. She'd baked the cookies for her class at school. Although only six years old, she loved sharing her skills with others. Hannah said, "Mommy, one boy is allergic to cookies. I want to bring him a piece of my candy that I saved."

"That's a great idea. He has an allergy to gluten, and that's in the flour in the cookies."

"We put a few cups of flour in the bowl when we made the cookies," Hannah said.

The teacher smiled when Hannah explained that she had a special treat for the class, including the student who couldn't eat cookies. The boy thanked Hannah and sucked on his treat while everyone else gobbled up the cookies. Hannah was thankful she'd remembered he had allergies.

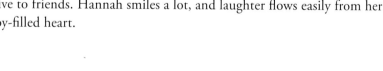

Hannah saved her birthday money and thought about what to spend it on. While shopping, her brother really wanted quarters for the candy machine. Hannah gave her brother quarters from her money. She also gave some of it to missionaries at church. She always did extra chores to earn more money to give.

Hannah learned to sew. She made a tiny pillow for her brother and little pillows for her aunts who loved cats. She often draws pictures to give to friends. Hannah smiles a lot, and laughter flows easily from her joy-filled heart.

Bible Story Connection 2 minutes

Put a few pennies on the table. Ask your children what you can do with them. Read about a poor widow who needed all her pennies for food, but gave them to God (Luke 21:1-3). Chat about giving more than just a little to God.

Chat Prompts: Options

"Those who give freely will be blessed. That's because they share their food with those who are poor." – Proverbs 22:9

Chat about giving freely from the heart without being asked to or encouraged by someone. Discuss ways to be generous at home with hugs, doing extra chores, and spending time helping a family member. How can you be generous with desserts or snacks? What can you do to help people who are poor and hungry?

MORE TIME?

"Give, and it will be given to you. A good amount will be poured into your lap. It will be pressed down, shaken together, and running over. The same amount you give will be measured out to you." – Luke 6:38

God reminds us that we're often blessed when we are generous. Discuss times you gave and then received something unexpected in return. Chat about the blessings of receiving smiles from people you help.

"Each of you should give what you have decided in your heart to give. You shouldn't give if you don't want to. You shouldn't give because you are forced to. God loves a cheerful giver." – 2 Corinthians 9:7

Talk about being cheerful when you give. What will you choose to give this week?

Scrapbook/Prayer Journal Options

Express your generosity by adding art to the pages of this book.

- Draw money and add places you've given help and money.

- Draw a piggy bank and write how much you plan to give from what you earn and save this month.

- Draw a heart with smiles to show you are a cheerful giver.

Prayer

Father, help us be grateful for our blessings. We want to be generous in all we do. We are willing to share and give from what you give us.

Wrap Up

Discuss ways family members gave generously this week. Chat about how God blessed you this week.

Following God

Family Beatitude: Happy is the family who responds to God's calls, for they will be his disciples.

Focus: Putting faith to work

Weekly Bible Verse: *"We all have gifts. They differ according to the grace God has given to each of us. Do you have the gift of prophecy? Then use it according to the faith you have."* – Romans 12:6

Activity Options on Following God

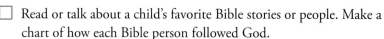

☐ Put together some jigsaw puzzles without looking at the picture of the finished puzzle. It can be hard to know what to do next. Chat about how knowing the will of God sometimes puzzles us, but we need to work at it one step at a time.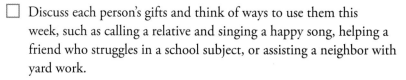

☐ Read or talk about a child's favorite Bible stories or people. Make a chart of how each Bible person followed God.

☐ Follow directions for a recipe to make something. Chat about how it's easy if you follow each step. Talk about how the Bible contains directions for following God.

☐ Discuss each person's gifts and think of ways to use them this week, such as calling a relative and singing a happy song, helping a friend who struggles in a school subject, or assisting a neighbor with yard work.

The Big Guy in Preschool

1-2 minutes

Michael said, "Mom, I want to volunteer to help in the preschool Sunday-school class."

"You might overwhelm those little ones. Why, you're almost six feet tall now, even if you are still a young teenager."

"I'll be gentle. My youth group talked about ways to serve at church with our gifts. I like little kids, and they seem to like me. I don't know what they do in the class, but I'm willing to help any way I can."

Michael spoke with the teachers. They also wondered about having "a giant" among the little ones, but they agreed to let him try. He started helping out, and the children loved him. They climbed on Michael and brought him books to read to them.

The teachers expressed their gratitude to Michael's mom. "We love having Michael help out. He has so much more energy than we do. Wow! He moves tables fast and cleans up toys quickly!"

Outside of class, when the children saw Michael they raced over and wrapped their arms around his knees. He'd bend down and listen to them, and then he'd hug them or rumple their hair. They didn't all remember his name, and sometimes one would point Michael out to their parents and say, "Look! That's the big guy in my class. He's my friend." The parents usually did a double take and then laughed as they realized their child's hero was actually a teenager.

Bible Story Connection 2 minutes

Read Micah 6:8. Talk about what God wants from you. Read the parable of "the Good Samaritan" in Luke 10:25-37. How did the Samaritan show humility, justice, and kindness? Talk about someone your family knows that could use some kindness. How can you show them God's love?

Chat Prompts: Options

"Do everything you say or do in the name of the Lord Jesus. Always give thanks to God the Father through Christ." – Colossians 3:17

God asks you to do everything in the name of Jesus. How does this help you look at your actions and make choices that please God?

MORE TIME?

The apostle Paul wrote, *"Follow my example, just as I follow the example of Christ."* – 1 Corinthians 11:1

Jesus wants us to follow his example. What are some things Jesus did? What examples will you follow?

"Be very careful how you live. Do not live like people who aren't wise. Live like people who are wise." – Ephesians 5:15

How can you live wisely? How can you make choices that help you follow Jesus? In what ways did you follow Jesus this week?

"I will make you into a great nation. And I will bless you. I will make your name great. You will be a blessing to others."
– John 15:5

God spoke these words to Abraham. He gave Abraham a simple task. He wanted him to be a blessing to others. How will you be a blessing to someone this week?

Scrapbook/Prayer Journal Options

Add art that shows how you follow God and show kindness and love to others.

- List ways you showed love and kindness this week. Make plans on how your family's acts of kindness can become a regular part of your week.

- Add mazes and puzzle shapes. Note how God usually lets his people know only a few things at a time about His will.

- Draw footprints and write down ways to follow God.

Prayer

Father, help me read the Bible and follow what it says. Remind me to talk to you. I want to know what you want me to do.

Wrap Up

Discuss opportunities you might have to follow Jesus this week.

Sharing Your Faith

Family Beatitude: Happy is the family that treasures God's Word, for they will know God treasures them.

Focus: Sharing your faith

Weekly Bible Verse: *"All the treasures of wisdom and knowledge are hidden in him."* – Colossians 2:3

Activity Options on Sharing Your Faith

☐ God wants us to share our faith. Help each child make a faith treasure box filled with reminders about Bible stories and prayer answers. Encourage them to use their boxes as a way to share their faith.

☐ Keep supplies on hand for your children to help their friends make faith treasure boxes.

☐ Make little booklets for children to draw or write a story about what God has done in his or her life.

☐ Take photos and scrapbook these special times of faith. These can include holy days, baptisms, church events, and times a child performs at church.

My Treasure Box 2 minutes

"Look at my special treasure box." Becky showed her decorated shoebox to her friend Nancy.

"See this feather? It's in my box because Jesus cares for the birds, and he cares for me too. Jesus said that."

Nancy picked up a curl of blond hair tied with a ribbon. "Why is some of your hair in the box?"

"That's because God loves me so much that he counts every hair on my head," Becky said. "Do you have a treasure box?"

Nancy shook her head.

Becky said, "I could help you make one."

The girls gathered paper, glue, old magazines, and a shoebox. They decorated the outside of the box with pictures of things God created. Then the girls looked for items to put into the box.

Nancy said she knew God loved her, so they cut a heart shape using folded paper. Nancy wrote, "God loves me!" on the heart and put it into the box.

Becky told Nancy some Bible stories, and they found items to go with the stories. For Noah's ark, they put in little animals they made from molding clay. Becky asked her mom for cinnamon sticks and ribbon. She helped Nancy tie the sticks together to form a cross and talked about how Jesus died for both of them.

They sang a song about a house built on sand and a house built on rock. Then they went outside. Each girl found a small rock to put into their boxes. They drew houses on the rocks with markers.

Becky kept her box on her dresser and showed it to her friends who visited.

Bible Story Connection

Read Hebrews 4:12 and portions of Psalm 119. The psalm reminds us why God's word is such a great treasure. Chat about why we should value God's Word.

Chat Prompts: Options

● *"You are a holy nation. The Lord your God has set you apart for himself. He has chosen you to be his special treasure. He chose you out of all the nations on the face of the earth."* – Deuteronomy 14:2

How are you God's treasure? In what ways do you treasure God?

MORE TIME?

● *"It had the golden altar for incense. It also had the wooden chest called the ark of the covenant. The ark was covered with gold. It held the gold jar of manna. It held Aaron's walking stick that had budded. It also held the stone tablets. The words of the covenant were written on them."* – Hebrews 9:4

The Ark of the Covenant was a special gold-covered box. It held three symbols to remind people of God. Chat about these treasures. Talk about the treasures you've received from God. How do these treasures make you rich in faith?

● *"[Jesus] said to them, 'Every teacher of the law who has become a disciple in the kingdom of heaven is like the owner of a house. He brings new treasures out of his storeroom as well as old ones.' "* – Matthew 13:52

What things do you treasure? What do you keep in your home that is special?

● Job said, *"I haven't disobeyed [God's] commands. I've treasured his words more than my daily bread."* – Job 23:12

Why is God's Word a treasure? What scriptures have you memorized? What Bible stories are your favorites?

Scrapbook/Prayer Journal Options

Add art to reflect what you find really worth treasuring.

- Draw a treasure box. Add hearts and write in family member names as a reminder that God treasures each person.

- Think about your favorite Bible stories and draw related items or symbols that could go inside a treasure box.

- Draw the items in the Ark of the Covenant that God wanted his people to treasure to remind them of their faith in him.

Prayer

Lord, thanks for treasuring us. Help us treasure you and your word and to each other this year.

Wrap Up

Discuss what each person treasures about God and your family.

Temptation and Sin

Family Beatitude: Happy is the family who learns to overcome temptation, for they will develop endurance.

Focus: Overcoming temptation

Weekly Bible Verse: *"Watch and pray. Then you won't fall into sin when you are tempted. The spirit is willing, but the body is weak."*

– Mark 14:38

Activity Options on Overcoming Temptation

☐ Talk about what tempts each person. Let each person follow these few steps: Write the problem down, list some ideas to help overcome the temptation, decide on what to do, and then take action. Post the plan where the person will see it.

☐ Make a heart guard. This could be an emblem or badge to wear. Add a scripture that will remind you to resist the temptation to lie, such as a stop sign to say no, a tongue depressor to control the tongue, or a soft pompon to encourage you to have a heart that is true.

☐ On days you resist temptation and do well, wear a crown or baseball cap with a cross on it as a reminder that God has a crown for people who successfully come through hard times relying on him.

Guilt Is *Not* Fun 1-2 minutes

"Mommy, I'm sorry I lied. I didn't do my work because I wanted to play my video games longer. But then it wasn't fun playing because I knew I'd lied to you."

"Joseph, you've always told the truth before this month. You know lying is a sin. You lied so you could have more time to play. As a consequence and punishment, we will take away two hours of your playtime."

Joseph nodded and said, "I understand. I'm sorry."

"I'm thankful you confessed. I forgive you, so I will give back half of the playtime I had to take away."

"Thank you, Mom. I know I have to stop lying, but I can't seem to. I have a hard time not thinking about my games and wanting to play. What can I do?"

Joseph's mom had her son write an essay about his problem. She asked him to come up with a few ideas on how to focus on always telling the truth.

After some thought, Joseph asked his mom to print up a picture of a suit of armor. He taped it by the TV to remind him he can be strong enough to fight temptation. His mom showed him Mark 14:38 in the Bible. He decided to write it out on a big piece of paper and taped it to his bedroom wall. Each morning it would remind him to pray and ask God to help him not be tempted to lie.

His mom gave him a high-five for such good ideas.

Bible Story Connection 2 minutes

Talk about what tempts each person and ways to not give in. Make a list of what each family member is tempted by. Pray for each other as a family to overcome temptation by asking God for help.

Chat Prompts: Options

- *"Put on all of God's armor. Then you can remain strong against the devil's evil plans."* – Ephesians 6:11

Take a look at Ephesians 6:10-18. What piece of armor will help each person with his or her biggest temptation?

MORE TIME?

- *"Blessed is the person who keeps on going when times are hard. After they have come through hard times, this person will receive a crown. The crown is life itself. The Lord has promised it to those who love him."* – James 1:12

Sometimes it's easier to get through a struggle by focusing on the reward. Talk about how rewards help motivate a person to be strong against temptation. What would be the reward for not watching a bad TV show? What could be a reward for taking a stand to not join a friend in a bad decision?

- *"Above everything else, guard your heart. Everything you do comes from it. Don't speak with twisted words. Keep evil talk away from your lips."* – Proverbs 4:23-24

What problems can talking cause? Discuss guarding your heart and making sure to control your mouth. How can you practice using your words for good?

Scrapbook/Prayer Journal Options

Use art to reinforce the ideas you've shared about defeating and overcoming temptation.

- Draw weapons that help you overcome temptation.

- Draw a "tongue of fire" to represent the Holy Spirit, and write a prayer for help to be strong.

- Draw a heart with a guard over it as a reminder to guard your heart.

Prayer

Lord Jesus, you died to save us from sin. We thank you for forgiving us. Help us be strong and overcome temptation with your help.

Wrap Up

Chat about praying for family members to have strength over their weaknesses. What decisions have each of you made to stand strong against temptation?

Making Decisions

Family Beatitude: Happy is the family who considers choices carefully, for they will make good decisions.

Focus: Making wise decisions

Weekly Bible Verse: King Solomon asked the Lord, *"Give me a heart that understands. Then I can rule over your people. I can tell the difference between what is right and what is wrong. Who can possibly rule over this great nation of yours?"* – 1 Kings 3:9

Activity Options on Making Decision

☐ As a family, look at an upcoming decision. Make a list of the pros and cons of the choices. Include costs and time needed. Consider how your family's talents and interests fit in.

☐ Evaluate outcomes of decisions. For purchases, check how long an item lasted and how much the person used it.

☐ Schedule a debate about an issue before an election. See what helps each person make a decision.

So Many Choices 1-2 minutes

"Boys, it's time to choose what sports and activities you want to do this fall. I have a list and some flyers of options. You can each choose one. If you both choose the same activity, then you can each choose a second one to do together."

Joyce knew she and her husband could only spend so much time driving their sons to activities. If they went to the same place, they had a little more time.

Bryan and Kyle flipped through the flyers. They each made a list of four activities they liked. They compared notes and saw that they both had listed soccer and the Lego team. Bryan also had football and scouts listed. Kyle had listed symphony and lacrosse.

Mom said, "This is the first time you've both listed two of the same activities."

They waited for Dad to get home, prayed as a family, and talked about what they liked about each activity listed. The boys liked sports because it helped them build muscles and play outside. Scouts included camping, while the symphony provided Kyle an opportunity to put his years of trumpet lessons to use. At last they decided to do the two activities they'd both listed. They would enjoy a sport and something that challenged their minds. They could each choose one of the other activities the next year.

Bryan said, "We can practice together too. That will be new."

Bible Story Connection 2 minutes

Read Luke 14:28-30. Imagine as a family, what might be needed to build a tower. Why is it important to figure out the cost before starting? What else do you need to know when you make a decision?

Chat Prompts: Options

● *"Trust in the Lord with all your heart. Do not depend on your own understanding. In all your ways obey him. Then he will make your paths smooth and straight."* – Proverbs 3:5-6

Decisions can be hard. What steps will you take when making important decisions? How can you trust your decisions to God? What choices have you made after praying first? How did that help?

MORE TIME?

● *"Solid food is for those who are grown up. They have trained themselves to tell the difference between good and evil. That shows they have grown up."* – Hebrews 5:14

Making decisions is part of growing up. Why does it take training? What do you do when you don't like a choice you made? How can you know the difference between good and evil?

● *"On one of those days, Jesus went out to a mountainside to pray. He spent the night praying to God. When morning came, he called for his disciples to come to him. He chose twelve of them and made them apostles."* – Luke 6:12-13

What did Jesus do before he chose His apostles? He began to make a decision by praying to God. What decisions do you need to pray about?

Scrapbook/Prayer Journal Options

Illustrate your thoughts on making decisions.

- Draw a balance scale and write ideas on how to make good choices.

- Draw various sports equipment, musical instruments, and other symbols of activities you might want to try.

- Draw a dollar sign and clock as symbols of costs and time involved with your choices.

Prayer

Father, guide us as we make decisions. Help us consider the positives and consequences so we will choose wisely.

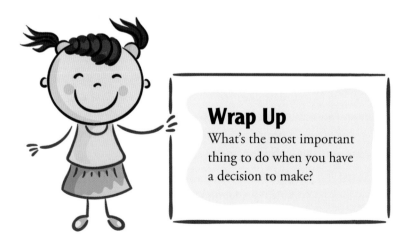

Wrap Up

What's the most important thing to do when you have a decision to make?

Thanksgiving

Family Beatitude: Happy is the family who is grateful, for they will be filled with joy.

Focus: Thankfulness

Weekly Bible Verse: *"Give thanks as you enter the gates of [God's] temple. Give praise as you enter its courtyards. Give thanks to him and praise his name."* – Psalm 100:4

Activity Options for Thanksgiving

- [ ] Use kernels of corn as symbols as you thank God for your blessings. Then pop some corn and marvel at how something small and hard transforms into something white and fluffy. God transforms hard times into blessings too.
- [ ] Plan activities to enjoy Thanksgiving Day or any day you want to give thanks, such as games and singing songs of thanksgiving. Choose hymns that express thanks.
- [ ] Decorate your table with a cornucopia or basket holding fruit and wheat and other autumn produce. Leave out papers for guests to write things they are thankful for, and encourage them to add these papers to the "horn of plenty."
- [ ] Fold autumn-colored paper in half. Then flatten and trace hands on the fold and refold to make booklets. Pass out markers or pens, and ask everyone to write or draw about blessings from God for which they are thankful.

FAMILY DEVOTION
• READ ALOUD •

Kernels of Thanks 1-2 minutes

Bella picked up two kernels of corn. Plop. She dropped one in the basket as she said, "Thank God for my family and friends." Plop. She dropped in the second one and said, "Thank God for helping me do well in school."

Bella's family members took turns thanking God for two blessings each as they dropped the kernels into a small basket. They gave thanks for their home, loved ones, jobs, and faith. They did this every year at Thanksgiving before they began eating the family meal.

Traditionally, Thanksgiving in America began with the pilgrims thanking God and some Native Americans for helping them survive their first year. They probably ate squash, corn, onions, fish, and deer cooked over outdoor fires. When the pilgrims set sail from England and finally landed in Plymouth, Massachusetts, William Bradford wrote:

Being thus arrived in a good harbor, and brought safe to land, they fell upon their knees and blessed the God of Heaven who had brought them over the vast and furious ocean, and delivered them from all the perils and miseries thereof, again to set their feet on the firm and stable earth, their proper element.

The harsh weather in New England made it difficult for the pilgrims. They survived, but only with the help of their Wampanoag friends. At the First Thanksgiving, they may have played games, such as the Indian game of "Ring the Pin" or the English game of "Blind Man's Bluff." They probably sang and danced. That made it a great feast and time of joy.

Bible Story Connection 2 minutes

Read Nehemiah 12:27, 43 to discover loud and joyful times of thanksgiving. The people, along with Nehemiah, celebrated the completion of the wall around Jerusalem and dedicated the wall to God. Put on praise music and sing, dance, and parade to it.

Chat Prompts: Options

● *"While they were eating, Jesus took bread. He gave thanks and broke it. He handed it to his disciples and said, 'Take this and eat it. This is my body.' "* – Matthew 26:26

Jesus thanked God often. This very special celebration Jesus started is sometimes called "Eucharist." That is a Greek word meaning "giving of thanks" or "thanksgiving." We also call it "Communion." Talk about Communion at your church.

MORE TIME?

● *"Celebrate the Feast of Weeks. Bring the first share of your crops from your fields. Celebrate the Feast of Booths. Hold it in the fall when you gather in your crops from your fields."*
– Exodus 23:16

God instructed the Israelites to celebrate different feasts and take time to thank him. One is the "Ingathering," also called "Sukkot" or the "Feast of Tabernacles," to rejoice at harvest in the fall. Discuss reasons to be thankful for a good harvest.

● *"Give thanks no matter what happens. God wants you to thank him because you believe in Christ Jesus."*
– 1 Thessalonians 5:18

Some days and even months can be very difficult, and it's hard to be thankful. God reminds us to be thankful at those times for Jesus and our faith. How can Jesus and thoughts of heaven help you be thankful when things go wrong?

Scrapbook/Prayer Journal Options

Add Thanksgiving symbols and words to your book.

- Draw kernels of corn and write about blessings God has given your family.

- Write out what you are thankful for.

- Draw about one of your family's Thanksgiving traditions.

Prayer

Father, thanks for all you have given us. Help us be grateful to you every day of the year.

Wrap Up

Chat about your favorite Thanksgiving foods and traditions. Talk about the blessings God gave you this year.

Failure

> **Family Beatitude:** Happy is the family who overcomes failure, for they will learn persistence.
>
> **Focus:** Perseverance
>
> **Weekly Bible Verse:** *"If you grow weak when trouble comes, your strength is very small!"* – Proverbs 24:10

Activity Options on Persistence

☐ Take photos related to a success each person had that took hard work. It might be riding a bicycle, reading, a science project, or tackling a new skill. Post them as reminders that persistence pays off.

☐ At the end of a bad day, pause and look for lessons learned and reasons to be grateful. List them. Thank God for getting you through tough days.

☐ Reframing something means to take the negative and state it as a positive challenge or to find a new, positive way to look at it. Put up a frame with a verse on persistence in it as a reminder to reframe difficult times.

☐ Cut a block from wood (or buy a block). Sand it. Draw or glue on pictures of "stumbling blocks" you've overcome and prayers that help you continue to try after failure.

FAMILY DEVOTION
• READ ALOUD •

A Terrible Day 1-2 minutes

"Dad, my science experiment didn't work. I wanted to show how to make a television since you made our TV set. It didn't work. Then I tried to grow mold, but that got too yucky. I've failed at everything! I have to turn in a project next week. What am I going to do?"

"There's still time, so don't give up. Let's talk about it later tonight. I need to make dinner right now."

Becky went downstairs and started watching a TV show. She smelled smoke and looked around. She yelled, "Dad, there's smoke coming out of the fuse box!"

Her father rushed down the stairs. "The fuse box?" Flames were coming out of the wall by the time he landed at the bottom of the steps. He grabbed a fire extinguisher. Swoosh! He put out the fire. He grabbed a cloth to protect his hand and yanked out the main fuse. Then he called the fire department. He asked Becky to go upstairs and show the firefighters the way to the basement when they arrived.

Smoke filled the downstairs. A firefighter checked the box and completely pulled it out of the wall.

"What a disaster. It's been a bad day," Becky said. "Maybe I should do my project on fire safety."

Dad responded, "Yes, you could do it on fuse boxes."

The next day, Becky hammered nails into a board. She added wiring and foil to demonstrate how a foil fuse could burn out if too much electricity passed through it. She decorated the board and explained fire safety with various fuses. She also displayed their burned-out fuse box.

Two weeks later, people strolled into the science fair, held their noses, and said, "Whew! It smells like something's burning in here!" Becky received an "A" on her project! Her dad worked with the insurance company to clean up the smoke damage and repair the wall and fuse box.

Bible Story Connection 2 minutes

Read Luke 5:1-11. These fishermen had fished all night and failed to catch any fish. But they obeyed Jesus when he told them to try again. This time they caught a huge amount of fish with their nets. When was the last project you thought was too hard? Talk about trying a project again—this time with God's help.

Chat Prompts: Options

● *"My body and my heart may grow weak. God, you give strength to my heart. You are everything I will ever need."* – Psalm 73:26
"I have learned the secret of being content no matter what happens. I am content whether I am well fed or hungry. I am content whether I have more than enough or not enough. I can do all this by the power of Christ. He gives me strength." – Philippians 4:12-13

Talk about how God gives you strength. List each person's problems he or she is working on now. Chat about how you can trust the problem to God and rely on him for the strength needed to keep persevering. Pray for each other for God's strength to succeed.

● *" 'Sir,' the man replied, 'leave it alone for one more year. I'll dig around it and feed it.' "* – Luke 13:8

This is from a parable Jesus told about a gardener who asked the owner of a tree that hadn't produced fruit to give him another year to fertilize it and care for it before removing it from the vineyard. Chat about what trying longer or harder after a failure teaches you.

● *"Don't worry about tomorrow. Tomorrow will worry about itself. Each day has enough trouble of its own."* – Matthew 6:34

Chat about failure, fear, and worry. Why doesn't worry help? What does help?

Scrapbook/Prayer Journal Options

Add art to illustrate the truths learned this week about failure and persistence.

- Draw a frame and write steps about how to "reframe" a problem.

- Draw a heart and write "Love never fails!" on it.

- Draw a few "stumbling" blocks. Write things that cause you to trip or fail, and then note ways to go around or remove those blocks.

Liam's Scrapbook

Prayer

Father, help us see beyond failure to persist and try again. With your guidance, we can look at a problem as a positive challenge to overcome with your help.

Wrap Up

How has each person persisted and worked to overcome a problem this week.

Thoughtfulness

Family Beatitude: Happy is the family who is thoughtful, for they will be considerate of each other and others.

Focus: Thoughtfulness in caring for people

Weekly Bible Verse: *"No one should look out for their own interests. Instead, they should look out for the interests of others."* – 1 Corinthians 10:24

Activity Options on Thoughtfulness

☐ Take names from an angel tree or simply choose an age to donate to a mission or toy drive. Add little surprises that might make a child smile. If it's not a traditional gift-giving time, talk to a local mission, women's shelter, or family shelter to see if they have children you can help.

☐ Be mindful of neighbors and friends who may be struggling due to finances or the loss of a loved one. Do something special to lift their spirits. Discuss how to be sensitive to people's feelings and giving anonymously.

☐ Teach children how to wrap gifts, make bows, and craft gift toppers to show special care.

☐ Keep cards received on special occasions. Draw one out each day and pray for the sender.

The Angel Tree 1-2 minutes

"Let's choose angels from the tree."

"But then the tree won't have any decorations. Why do we want to take them off?" asked Lisa.

"Each angel has an age, a gender, and a suggested gift for someone who is in need. These are children who need people to care enough to buy them Christmas gifts or they might not get any," Mom answered.

"Oh. That's sad. Can we find a girl my age? Everyone should be happy at Christmas."

"Here's one. She wants jeans."

Lisa's family collected several angel slips and went into a nearby store. They read the age, gender, and what the person needed. The family shopped for jeans, coats, sweaters, and other items.

At home, Lisa said, "Daddy, I know this girl needs jeans, but I want to give her something more fun like a toy."

"Maybe we can fill the pockets with little surprises," he suggested.

"Yes! We can also add a note or Christmas card. We can pray for her too. Maybe next year she will have everything she needs."

"Those are great ideas. But, remember, we don't want to include our names. This is a secret way to help people. It's between God and us."

Lisa's family added money, small gift certificates, costume jewelry, a tiny doll, and other surprises to the different clothing items. They wrapped the gifts and used the paper angels as gift tags. Later they took the wrapped gifts to the angel tree and left them there as instructed.

Bible Story Connection **2 minutes**

Read Luke 7:36-48. Jesus praises a woman for being thoughtful and scolds a man for being inconsiderate. Jesus knows when we really are grateful for his love in our life. We show that love of God when we care for others. How did the woman in the story show how much she loved Jesus?

Chat Prompts: Options

● *"Even pull out some stalks for her. Leave them for her to pick up. Don't tell her she shouldn't do it."* – Ruth 2:16

Boaz owned a field where Ruth was gleaning or picking up grain left after harvesting. Boaz noticed Ruth and knew she and her mother-in-law were struggling to get by. He directed his men to leave extra wheat out so Ruth wouldn't have to work so hard to get enough food. What can you do to help people in need this week? Are you buying gifts for someone on an angel tree? If so, will you also pray for the person's family?

MORE TIME?

● *"The next day we landed at Sidon. There Julius was kind to Paul. He let Paul visit his friends so they could give him what he needed."* – Acts 27:3

Julius, a Roman soldier, guarded Paul, who was under arrest and being taken to Rome. Instead of being mean, the soldier chose to be kind, even letting Paul visit with friends and allowing him to accept their gifts. Talk about ways to think of others who need your help, such as the homeless or those less fortunate. What can you do this week to help?

● *"Blessed are those who care about weak people. When they are in trouble, the Lord saves them."* – Psalm 41:1

What do you do to help weak or needy people?

Scrapbook/Prayer Journal Options

Add art to reflect ways you can be thoughtful and considerate.

- Draw a gift as a reminder to surprise people with your thoughtfulness.

- Draw grain on stalks as a reminder of Boaz taking care to help Ruth get enough food.

- Draw an angel as a reminder to be a secret messenger of joy for people who need help.

Prayer

Lord, help us be thoughtful and consider people's needs and feelings. We want to act on our good thoughts and help others.

Wrap Up

Talk about how family members showed consideration this week.

Stress

Family Beatitude: Happy is the family who handles stress well, for they will be patient.

Focus: Handling stress well

Weekly Bible Verse: *Jesus said, "I leave my peace with you. I give my peace to you. I do not give it to you as the world does. Do not let your hearts be troubled. And do not be afraid."* – John 14:27

Activity Options on Handling Stress Well

- [ ] Practice de-stressing activities together, such as deep, slow breathing and jumping jacks. Make a list of activities that help each person relax and dissipate stressful energy.

- [ ] Check each child's calendar and activities. If it is so full that it causes stress, work on balancing activities, schoolwork, and chores. Make sure there is time to relax.

- [ ] Check the pantry and refrigerator. Chat about what foods are healthy and how good eating habits keep people healthy and help them handle stress better.

- [ ] Create an environment where it's easy to relax. Set up a prayer corner where children can go to pray and listen to God. Have comfortable couches or floor pillows. Have quiet music available to listen to that might help a person calm down.

Reading Stress 1-2 minutes

Elizabeth started crying when reading time came, and, as usual, her mother tried to calm her. Reading time often started this way—with a child's cry and a mom's raised voice. Stress invaded their togetherness.

One day Elizabeth's mom called her sister, who was a teacher. "What can I do about Elizabeth?" she asked. They decided to have Elizabeth visit her aunt for a week to see if she needed some special help reading.

Without making it a big deal, Aunt Becky tested Elizabeth's reading level when she arrived, before playing games and going to bed. Then, each morning, Aunt Becky gave Elizabeth a very easy book to read to start the day with a success. Elizabeth spent ten minutes reading. Smiled because she could do it easily. Aunt Becky smiled too. She let Elizabeth choose a sticker her mom had sent to use as rewards.

Later each morning, Elizabeth and her aunt read together, choosing a book a little above Elizabeth's reading level. Her aunt coached Elizabeth to sound out the harder words.

In the afternoon, Aunt Becky gave Elizabeth a book to read at her actual level that would still challenge her with a few new words. She gave Elizabeth time to read the book alone and then had Elizabeth read it aloud. Afterward, they discussed what the book said.

Elizabeth's mom and sister spoke on the phone. They made a new reading plan for Elizabeth. When Elizabeth returned home, her mom explained the new plan. She included Aunt Becky's plan of starting with an easy book that would end in hugs instead of tears. Reading time became fun.

Bible Story Connection **2 minutes**

Put out some bandages. Read Luke 8:43-48. Discuss the stress of being sick for a long time. Chat about how the healing took away the woman's stress and also healed her heart and mind. Talk about the fact that bandages don't always stop bleeding. People my need stitches or a doctor's help. Talk about how Jesus can heal any problem.

Chat Prompts: Options

"My brothers and sisters, you will face all kinds of trouble. When you do, think of it as pure joy." – James 1:2

God doesn't promise we will be happy every day and that everything will be great all the time. He knows we will face problems, and that they will help us grow. He knows we will have sadness that will help us understand ourselves and other people better. But we get to choose our attitude. How can you choose to trust God is in charge and be happy? Talk about your attitude when problems arise. What steps you can take to trust God and not stress?

MORE TIME?

"Can you add even one hour to your life by worrying?"
– Luke 12:25

Jesus spoke these words during what we call the "Sermon on the Mount." He also pointed out that flowers and birds don't worry, and God takes care of them. He told people to seek God and not focus on their problems. Chat about how worry doesn't help. Also talk about how to turn thinking around to make a problem a positive challenge or goal instead of a worry. Help each person reframe a worry as a positive challenge.

"Never stop praying." – 1 Thessalonians 5:17

Chat about the power of prayer and how God will help you feel better. Have each person list the stresses they have and stop and pray for each other. Promise to continue to pray.

Scrapbook/Prayer Journal Options

Add art as reminders to stress less, talk to God more, and face problems with hope.

- Draw healthy snacks. Write how eating healthy foods helps a person handle stress better.

- Draw praying hands and write problems on the fingers as a reminder to give your worries to God.

- Draw an hourglass and write how to choose to use your moments wisely instead of worrying.

Prayer

Father, help us talk to you about our problems. We want to have good attitudes and face challenges with hope because you are on our side.

Wrap Up

Chat about a problem that caused stress for each person and what that person did to lessen the stress.

Fairness and Justice

> **Family Beatitude:** Happy is the family who understands fairness, for they will be content.
>
> **Focus:** Fairness
>
> **Weekly Bible Verse:** *"Do to others as you want them to do to you."*
> – Luke 6:31

Activity Options on Fairness

☐ Paint a ruler gold. Write "Treat others how you want to be treated" on it. Display this "Golden Ruler" as a reminder of how to relate to people.

☐ Hold a family meeting. Chat about family rules and how to treat each other. List some rules that will help remind you to treat each other fairly (good manners, sharing, taking turns, and so forth).

☐ Let children take turns dividing food. Make sure the child understands that he or she will serve the food, and everyone else gets to choose first. This helps children divide evenly.

FAMILY DEVOTION • READ ALOUD •

What's Fair? 1-2 minutes

"Mom, I've been thinking. You spend a lot more money on Emma's dance than on my soccer. That's not fair," complained Ethan.

Mom replied, "Well, I can do the same for you."

"Great! I have plans on how to spend the extra money."

"No, I meant I will pay for you to take dance lessons too. And I will ask Emma if she wants to play soccer."

"That's not what I meant."

"It's fair that we help you each do what you want to do. Soccer costs less because our taxes help pay for the program. The dance program is private, so there is no public funding and it costs more."

"So being fair doesn't mean spending equal money?"

"In our family, fair is choosing what is best for each person. It's also about following 'the Golden Rule.' "

"The 'Golden Rule'?"

"Yes. Jesus told us to treat people the way we want to be treated. For example, you speak politely, share desserts, and take turns choosing games to play to treat others well."

"Is God fair?"

"God is 'just.' It's not about being equal. God made each of us unique. He chose your blue eyes and my green eyes. He has a plan for each of us, and the plans are not identical. He doesn't want us to compare ourselves to each other. He wants us to use the talents He gives to follow Him and His plans for us."

"So I won't get extra money, but you'll let me do things I like to do. I can live with that."

"That's right. Now, how would you like me to take you for some ice cream?"

"Great! I want mint chocolate chip."

212

Bible Story Connection 2 minutes

Put out a gavel or small hammer and a small block of wood. Read Luke 18:1-8. A widow continually sought justice from a judge, but he refused to help her. The widow made more complaints and persisted. Finally the judge relented and helped her.

A judge knocks loudly with his gavel to get attention. Hit the block of wood with the hammer and talk about what happens in your family when decisions are made. Is there a time frame? When can they be reconsidered? Are consequences negotiable?

Chat Prompts: Options

● *"Are you jealous? Are you concerned only about getting ahead? Then your life will be a mess. You will be doing all kinds of evil things. But the wisdom that comes from heaven is pure. That's the most important thing about it. And that's not all. It also loves peace. It thinks about others. It obeys. It is full of mercy and good fruit. It is fair. It doesn't pretend to be what it is not."* – James 3:16-17

When do you think of what you want first? Practice finding opportunities to put others first this week. Be sure to praise your family when you see them putting others first.

MORE TIME?

● *"Speak up and judge fairly. Speak up for the rights of those who are poor and needy."* – Proverbs 31:9

How can you think beyond what you want so you will speak up for other people? How can you help people in need this week?

● *"Someone in the crowd spoke to Jesus. 'Teacher,' he said, 'tell my brother to divide the family property with me.'"* – Luke 12:13

Jesus didn't tell the brother to divide the property. Instead, He responded to the complainer's heart. He spoke about avoiding greed and mentioned life is not about how much stuff we own (verse 15). Chat about these ideas.

Scrapbook/Prayer Journal Options

Add artwork that reinforces concepts of fairness and justice.

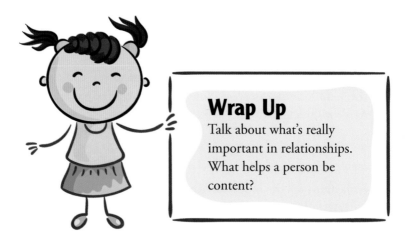

- Draw a ruler and color it gold. Write down ideas of how people want to be treated.

- Draw different-colored eyes. Add words about being unique and how it's important for each person to follow his or her own path and not look at what other people do or receive.

- Make a praise list of family you saw putting others first.

Prayer

Lord, help us be content. Remind us to treat people the way we want to be treated.

Wrap Up

Talk about what's really important in relationships. What helps a person be content?

Celebrating Jesus

Family Beatitude: Happy is the family who knows Jesus is the reason for Christmas, for they will praise God.

Focus: Celebrating Jesus

Weekly Bible Verse: *"God so loved the world that he gave his one and only Son. Anyone who believes in him will not die but will have eternal life."* – John 3:16

Activity Options for Celebrating Jesus

☐ Consider using Christmas stockings or other traditions to help focus on the reason Jesus came. For stockings, contents might include:
  - fruits that represent the fruit of the Spirit
  - toy vehicles as reminders to go and tell people about Jesus
  - sweet treats as reminders that God's Word is sweeter than honey, and the news about Jesus is one of the sweetest gifts God gives

☐ Celebrate with a cake for the birth of Jesus. Sing Christmas carols.

☐ Turn your Christmas tree into a reminder of God's eternal love. Read Hosea 14:8, where God compares himself to an evergreen tree. God made trees, and they are the longest known living organisms on earth.

☐ Use a nativity set to focus on Jesus. Let each person take one figure (or draw the name of a figure) from the set. Have each person talk about the importance of that figure in the birth of Jesus.

Filled with Christmas Spirit 1-2 minutes

Everyone gathered around a lit candle. Dad read from the Bible about the birth of Jesus and then they sang "Happy Birthday" to Him. They grabbed their stockings stuffed with treasures and sat down.

Logan, the youngest, took the first turn. He drew out a pack of batteries. He said, "The Holy Spirit gives us power."

When Hailey's turn came, she pulled out a heart necklace. "A heart is for love. Jesus came because He loves us and wants us to be in heaven with Him."

A little later, Dad held up a cross to put on his car antenna. "He came as a little baby, but we know He had a purpose. He would grow up and die on a cross to save us. Jesus fills our hearts with love."

The stocking tradition continued as each one connected a spiritual message with a surprise from the stocking. Through the various thoughts, they talked about the reason why Jesus came, God's love, and being filled with the Holy Spirit. No one rushed to reveal all the contents of the

stockings. It took quite a while with seven people in the family, but the tradition helped them focus on the true reason for celebrating Christmas.

After going through the stockings, the family opened presents, enjoyed visits from friends, and ended the day singing carols.

Bible Story Connection 2-3 minutes

Read about the birth of Jesus in Matthew 1:18-25 and Luke 2:1-21. Pass around a baby doll and discuss how the birth of Jesus changed the world.

Chat Prompts: Options

- ""*Today in the town of David a Savior has been born to you. He is the Messiah, the Lord.*" – Luke 2:11

  Angels told shepherds about the birth of Jesus. They were humble men; in fact, shepherds were looked down upon by many people back then. By telling them first God was saying Jesus had come for all people no matter their position. We are to view all people through the loving eyes of God. How can this impact how we think? What are some people in the world that are treated as less important or ignored? How can you show love to them?

MORE TIME?

- *"Give praise to the Lord, the God of Israel! He has come to his people and purchased their freedom."* – Luke 1:68

  What does it mean he came and purchased our freedom? If you have more time look up Romans 6:23 and Romans 3:22-25. Why did Jesus come? What did he do for you?

- ""*They asked, 'Where is the child who has been born to be king of the Jews? We saw his star when it rose. Now we have come to worship him.'*" - Matthew 2:2

  The wise men followed a star to find Jesus. They stopped at the palace of King Herod, but they didn't find him there. At last they came to Bethlehem and worshipped Jesus. Discuss the wonder of these foreign scholars understanding signs that God sent and recognizing Jesus as God's chosen King of his people.

217

Scrapbook/Prayer Journal Options

Add decorations and symbols that reflect your reason for celebrating Christmas.

- Add angels, shepherds, and people who knew about the birth of Jesus.

- Draw stockings, musical instruments, and wreaths. Write notes about how they remind you of why Jesus came.

- Add a crown for Jesus, the newborn King, and draw a cross on it for what Jesus came to do.

Prayer

Father God, thank you for sending Jesus to save us. Thank you, Jesus, for coming and opening the gates of heaven for us.

Wrap Up

Discuss what Christmas means to you, especially this year.

Winter Fun

Family Beatitude: Happy is the family who explores winter wonders, for they will be awed by God's power and creation.

Focus: Appreciating winter

Weekly Bible Verse: *"When it snows, she's not afraid for her family. All of them are dressed in the finest clothes."* – Proverbs 31:21

Activity Options for Winter Fun

☐ Make the most of a snowy day with sledding or creating snow people or snow animals. Make sure to have warm drinks or soup to help you warm up afterward. Discuss frostbite and how to prevent it.

☐ If you don't have snow in your area, make some fake snow: Cut open a disposable diaper and scoop out the powder. It is sodium acrylate. Add a little water, and it will feel cool to the touch. Make it sparkle by adding white or clear glitter.

☐ Plan a winter scavenger hunt. Children can take photos of some objects and collect other items. Depending on the weather, you can include: bare trees, gloves, mittens, dead leaves, evergreen trees, animal tracks, dead grass, ice, bird nests, leaves clinging to a tree, snow, socks.

Snow Fun and Cocoa 1-2 minutes

"Mommy, it's snowing! Hooray! No school today."

Ethan and his family looked out the window to see how the world had changed overnight. The white-covered trees and ground glistened. Already friends had bundled up and started making tunnels and snow people. Four feet of snow blanketed the yards and streets.

Ethan pulled on his snow pants, coat, gloves, woolen snow mask, scarf, and boots. He headed outside. The bigger boys and girls had dug tunnels and created towers. They invited him to crawl inside and explore the snow fort. He had fun standing in the towers and looking out at the winter wonderland.

Ethan's mom lay on the snow and fanned her arms and legs out to show him how to make a snow angel. He made a few angels and then trudged around trying to get through drifts that stood higher than his waist. After an hour, they returned home with icy-cold toes, fingers, and noses. They enjoyed steaming hot cocoa with marshmallows.

"I'm warming up, Mom," Ethan said. "Thanks for the snow pants, boots, and other things so I could play in the snow."

"You're welcome."

"It's so white and sparkly outside."

"Yes. God uses snow to remind us he can change things. He can change hearts too, and he can wash away our sins to make our hearts pure again."

"So I sparkle on the inside?"

"Yes."

Bible Story Connection 2 minutes

Read Hebrews 10:24-25. Each season brings special opportunities for fun, but the entire year has given your family an opportunity to have fun and grow in the Lord together. Discuss what you've enjoyed about meeting together and what your favorite times were. Look through your scrapbook/prayer journal and reflect on what you did together. What prayer requests did you see answered? Consider what you want to do as a family for the coming year to grow stronger in the Lord as individuals and as a family.

Chat Prompts: Options

"The law of the Lord is perfect. It gives us new strength. The laws of the Lord can be trusted. They make childish people wise."

– Psalm 19:7

Children make mistakes because they are still learning what is wise to do. Some adults make mistakes because they choose not to learn. God's Word gives us strength to do what is right and helps us grow wiser. Chat about how your family has grown closer, stronger, and wiser because of your time in God's Word.

MORE TIME?

"'Come. Let us settle this matter,' says the Lord. 'Even though your sins are bright red, they will be as white as snow. Even though they are deep red, they will be white like wool.'"

– Isaiah 1:18

How does the world look after it snows? How do you feel after you are forgiven? How is it easier to forgive other people when you know God forgives you? Talk about taking time each evening to review the day and ask God to forgive you for anything you've done wrong.

Scrapbook/Prayer Journal Options

Use art to add images of winter and helping to your book.

- Draw snowflakes and icicles. Add words about the cold and how you can help someone get warm.

- Draw snow people and write about God forgiving your sins and washing you as white as snow.

- Draw a mug of cocoa and write about warming up with family after playing in the snow.

Prayer

Lord, thank you for the cold season of winter and the wonder of nature. Help us seek your forgiveness when we need it.

Wrap Up

Congratulations! You've completed this family study guide. Chat about some of the best things you did and learned as you grew stronger together. Talk about what plans you have to continue family devotion time next year.

 # New for Parents

New! On the Go Family Devotions: First Steps Together

The Only Devotional Made Just For Families with Babies and Toddlers Ages 0-2

Ages 0–2, 224 pages, 5½"x 8½" Paperback, Full Color Illustrations, Retail $16.99

On The Go Family Devotions: First Steps Together serves as a roadmap for a parent's spiritual journey with their baby or toddler. *First Steps Together* removes the obstacles holding parents back from spiritually parenting their children by presenting 52 simple, structured devotionals. The peaceful tone and honest stories will create an atmosphere parents want to return to and continue. Parents will feel equipped and well cared for on their journey, as they develop a strong sense of confidence in their ability to guide their child to God and listen to the Holy Spirit.

| On the Go: First Steps Together | L50005 | 9781628625004 | $16.99 |

It is a great child and baby dedication gift for new parents.

New! On the Go Family Devotions: Journeying Together

A Devotional for Families with Children Ages 3-10

Ages 3–10, 224 pages, 5½"x 8½" Paperback, Full Color Illustrations, Retail $16.99

On The Go Family Devotions: Journeying Together takes the framework introduced in Deuteronomy 6 and applies to the daily life in the modern family. Each devotional gives parents ways to share their faith at home, on the road, when they wake up, and before they go to sleep. Each week, parents will engage in a devotion that centers them in Scripture and creates habits of engaging in casual conversations about God that will propel their child forward in their spiritual journey.

| On the Go: Journeying Together | L50006 | 9781628625011 | $16.99 |

RØSEKiDZ New for Parents

New! The Children's Rhyming Bible

When a story rhymes, kids want to hear it all the time!

Ages 3–7, 72 pages, 8"x 7" Hardcover, Full Color Illustrations, Retail $14.99

Capture and keep your kids' attention with this beloved Children's Rhyming Bible. Featuring joyful illustrations, vivid colors, and a bouncing beat, this beloved Rhyming Bible tells 34 popular Bible stories in an engaging and unforgettable way.

From Creation and Noah's Ark to Jesus' Birth and Resurrection, boys and girls will love the delightful rhymes that will stick in their minds and help them hide God's Word in their hearts. Each Bible story is short, easy-to-read, and stays accurate to the Bible. Perfect for reading aloud to younger children, bedtime stories, or even for older children wanting to read the Bible to themselves.

The Children's Rhyming Bible	L50004	9781628624991	$14.99

New! God and Me! 52 Week Devotional for Girls

384–386 pages, 6"x 9" Softcover, Full Color Illustrations, Retail $14.99

This devotional made for girls ages 6–9 and 10-12 covers situations you deal with at school and at home. Enjoy fully illustrated devotions as you are encouraged to rely on God by learning more about Him, His Word, and His plans for your life. Our unique 52-week devotional contains devotions and prayers on Days 1 through 5, and fun activities at the end of the week to reinforce the week's key Scripture memory verse and theme. Each day is designed to help you draw close to God.

Ages 6-9	L46838	978-1-584111-77-1	$14.99
Ages 10-12	L46839	978-1-584111-78-8	$14.99